Not a
Silent People

Controversies That Have Shaped Southern Baptists

To
Sherry, Paula, and Walt

Not a Silent People

Controversies That Have Shaped Southern Baptists

Walter B. Shurden

Smyth & Helwys Publishing, Inc.®
Macon, Georgia

ISBN 1-57312-021-9

Not a Silent People
Controversies That Have Shaped Southern Baptists

Walter B. Shurden

Copyright © 1995
Smyth & Helwys Publishing, Inc.
6316 Peake Road
Macon, Georgia 31210-3960
1-800-747-3016

Library of Congress Cataloging-in-Publication Data

Shurden, Walter B.
    Not a silent people: controversies that have shaped Southern Baptists/
    Walter B. Shurden.
        x + 118 pp.   6" x 9" (15 x 23 cm.)
        Includes bibliographical references.
        ISBN 1-57312-021-9
        1. Baptists—Doctrines—History.
        2. Southern Baptist Convention—Doctrines—History.
        3. Church controversies—Baptists—History.
        I. Title.
        BX6331.2.S53 1995
        286'.132—dc20   95-24170
                                                                    CIP

Contents

Preface to the Updated Edition

I outlined the original chapters for this book after a class session on Baptist history under Professor Claude L. Howe, Jr., at New Orleans Baptist Theological Seminary in 1960. I published the book twelve years later in 1972, now over two decades ago. For the last twenty-three years, Baptist ministers have used it to teach the Baptist heritage to their churches, campus ministers have used it with their students, and even college and seminary professors have used it in their classrooms. I have been both surprised and gratified at its popularity. The single most satisfying aspect of its wide usage for me has to do with the numerous lay people who have indicated that it gave them their first enjoyable taste of Baptist history.

This edition updates rather than revises the original. While I might would have preferred to revise some of the original chapters, I thought it best to leave them essentially as first written. Therefore, I have made only three changes in this edition. (1) The second preface is, of course, new. (2) I have corrected some minor printing errors and utilized gender-free language. My sins regarding the latter issue proved so egregious, however, I am sure that stains remain. Even the changes I have made would have been virtually impossible without the enormous help of Scott Nash and Jackie Riley of Smyth & Helwys Publishers. (3) I have added chapter seven, something requested of me for years. As most readers would understand, the real purpose of this updated edition is to tell the story of the most recent Southern Baptist controversy. At the Southern Baptist Convention in Houston, Texas, where the controversy began in 1979, Albert McClellan said to me, "Walter, it looks like you are going to have to add a chapter to *Not A Silent People*." Numerous people have urged me to do this since that time.

I am especially grateful that Cecil Staton, Scott Nash, Ron Jackson, and Jim Pitts had the courage to estabish Smyth & Helwys Publishing Company in 1990. They have provided for Baptists everywhere a free press. Nancy Stubbs, administrative secretary for the Christianity Department at Mercer University, was immensely helpful in preparing this manuscript for publication.

Spring 1995

Preface 1972

My wife, reared a non-Baptist, was a bit taken back when she got an inside look into Baptist churches. The thing that struck her was the amount of fussin' and fightin' that goes on there. But to her it was a sign of life, vitality, and concern. She declared on one occasion that she did not know that religious groups "cared enough to argue over anything." My response was, "If religious controversy is an index of how much people care, then Baptists care more than any group in the world."

Sometimes we Baptists have argued over major issues, and then again we have become vocal over trivia. But whether big or small, necessary or unnecessary, profitable or profitless, our denominational controversies have shaped us. We can't get away from their influence.

I really have three purposes for my Baptist readers. If you are not a Baptist, I believe you will see the advantages of my writing directly to my brothers and sisters in this book. One, I want to try to "turn Baptists on" to the denominational heritage. This means that I have tried to avoid the heavy hand of the historian. Pedantry is no virtue; yet, for the historian, even pedantry is not as great a vice as inaccuracy. I wanted to avoid both. Two, I want to show how our Baptist past affects us today. Three, and more indirectly, I hope you find in these pages some reasons why you who are Baptist can be grateful for being so. If you are not a Baptist, I hope you will find the following pages worth reading—for reasons that will become apparent later.

Most of the following chapters were first published in *The Student* in a somewhat revised form during 1970–1971. I am grateful that Norman Bowman, editor of *The Student*, believes that our denominational heritage matters and that students ought to be exposed to it.

I have also had a good time sharing these pages with two local Baptist congregations. I taught these Baptist controversies in the College Department Sunday School at Broadway Baptist Church in Knoxville, Tennessee. This is supposed to be the "now" generation, bloated with the present, anti-historical, and all that. I didn't find it to be true with these young people, however. Sherwood Baptist Church of Albany, Georgia also heard some of these addresses. It was my second visit to Sherwood to preach and teach history. That congregation did me the pleasure of acting interested.

Three people are due thanks. W. Morgan Patterson, professor of church history at Southern Baptist Theological Seminary, and Claude L. Howe, Jr., professor of church history at New Orleans Baptist Theological Seminary, read the manuscript and made helpful suggestions. Of course they are not responsible for any mistakes I made. Kay, my wife, not only typed the manuscript, but stayed up late at night acting interested in the excerpts I read her from "old" Baptist books.

Nothing can be understood until you know its history. For that reason, the Baptist heritage matters. Someone asked Leon McBeth, Baptist church historian, "What have Baptists ever done that they should deserve a history?" So he wrote an article entitled, "Do Baptists Deserve a History?" Naturally he answered with a "yes." So do I.

Walter B. Shurden

Introduction

"Here Come the Battling Baptists"

I do not know who wrote it or when or where or what the circumstances were, but it reeks with pessimism. Here is the poem:

> Our fathers have been churchmen
> 1900 years or so
> And to every new suggestion
> They always answered no.

If you listen attentively in religious circles, you may hear less poetic versions of the same theme. I once heard a forty-five year old Baptist deacon say that the seven most famous words in Baptist churches were, "We never did it that way before." A student—one of those intelligent, talented kind who was in holy revolt against his religious upbringing—echoed the same song. He was stalking (and stalking *is* the word for this irate one) out of a Baptist Student Union State Convention. What the student described as a denominational "bigee" had just finished a rousing thirty-minute sermon in which he called for allegiance to the status quo. I then heard the stalking one put the poetry into prose. "My! My! My!" he said, "The more things change, the more Baptists remain the same." I thought in the historical half of my mind: "Hasn't always been so!"

If you think that Baptists of today are devoted establishmentarians, if you see them as a herd of timid, effete thumb-sucking Christians, fearful of any controversy and all change, I have two suggestions for you. One, you may be wrong, but this is not the place to argue that point. Two, even if you are right about the "now" Baptists, do not make the mistake of thinking that Baptists have always been domesticated.

Baptists were born in the bosom of radicalism! They are born fighters because they were born fighting. As a distinct denomination, Baptists first began in seventeenth-century England. Label the religious parties of that period and here is what you come up with: Anglicans (English Episcopalians) were the "conservatives"; Puritans were the "liberals"; Quakers, Congregationalists, and Baptists were the "radicals"! Think of that! Baptists were not among the conservatives, wanting to maintain status quo.

They were not even among the *avant garde* liberals who wanted to tamper with the status quo and change it a little. They were among the radicals who wanted to reverse the religious establishment. That, reader friend, is a heady heritage—one that many Baptists have never learned, or else one they learned and conveniently forgot. Either way, it is a tragic misuse of history.

Churches—like any type of organization or society—are very much akin to children. Babies are eager for new experiences. Unchained by crusty habits and molded attitudes, they are free and willing to try anything once! There was a time when Baptists were babies—flexible, open, courageous infants of God! They would try anything once—or so it seemed to their opposition.

I

You probably never will but if someday during your leisure time you decide to write an historical essay on early Baptists, Gordon Kingsley has a suggestion for you: A good place to begin your research is in the records of court proceedings, search warrants, and prison records. Baptist names are written large there. The seventeenth century in England was a virtual hurricane of political and religious change. It was a disordered society. Baptists were looked upon "as chief culprits in the disorder of state and church."[1]

Baptists were the "agitators" of the seventeenth century. They were called, however, by even less complimentary names such as a "base sect," a "scab or error," a "seduced and . . . schismatical rabble of deluded children, servants, and people," "a profane and sacrilegious sect," "an impure and carnal sect," and like most who dare to question the sanctity of things-as-they are, Baptists were dubbed "anarchists." One of the opponents of our Baptist forebears said that "if this sect prevaile, we shall have no Monarchie in the State, nor Hierarchie in the Church, but an Anarchie in both."[2] He made a mistake!

Could a group so maligned by people in high places be innocent? Just how many horns did our devilish ancestors have? What was the nature of their sins? Judged by their times, Baptists in both England and America during the 1600s could be accused of two gross errors. One was theological; the other was political. Both involved a heretical way of thinking and an obnoxious way of acting, or so thought their adversaries.

Baptists were theological heretics because they dared to believe—and to say it out loud—that one could not be born or baptized into Christianity. *Christian discipleship is a style of living that involves choice—voluntary, conscious commitment.* Baptists developed from that theological axiom. The implication was clear enough: Infant baptism had to go—not primarily because the infants were sprinkled, but because the infants were infants! Baptists' first concern regarding baptism was not the *mode* of baptism, whether immersion, sprinkling or pouring. Their first concern was the *subject* of baptism. Their concern that the subject of baptism be capable of consciously choosing to be baptized appeared as stark heresy to the tradition of infant baptism.

The Establishment (in this case, the Church of England) began to cry for "religious law and order." "You are destroying the Church of Christ and everything that is holy!" screamed the panic-stricken Anglicans. (You probably have observed, as did John W. Gardner,[3] that a common strategy for resisting the swirling currents of change is to stand on high moral ground and assert that the old way is bound up with what is moral and spiritual. That was the Anglican plan, too.) "Humbug," blurted back the Baptists, "we are not destroying the Church of Christ; we are restoring it!"

Baptists contended that to demand a regenerate church membership, made up of believers only, would not damage the church; it would only declare the real nature of the church. They therefore pulled out of the Church of England and became "dissenters," emphasizing a "gathered" rather than a "parish" church. A "gathered" church was made up of people who voluntarily united in Christian fellowship. One had to *decide* to join the gathered church, not so with the parish church. One was a member of a parish church by virtue of involuntary baptism as an infant.

Describing the Baptists, one brilliant interpreter of Baptist life and thought said, "Their distinctive feature is the doctrine of the Church: that it must consist wholly of people who have pledged themselves to Christ Jesus."[4] That was Baptists' first instance of breaking with theological tradition, but it was certainly not the only place where they bucked the church forebears.[5]

By seventeenth-century ground rules, Baptists were far more than theological deviates; they were also political traitors. As a matter of fact, most British people of this period considered theological dissent from the Church of England tantamount to political treason to the State of

England. This was a scrambled-eggs society. Church and state came on the same plate and all mixed together! Baptists tried to unscramble the political-ecclesiastical eggs, maintaining that the State has no say-so over the soul of a person.

Some great free soul of history, who is yet anonymous to me, is supposed to have said something to the effect: "To cram a creed down a person's throat is rape of the soul!" Baptists agreed. but they went on to say that for the State to do the creed-cramming is to compound the assault. John Smyth, often called the first Baptist, spoke for all Baptists when he said, "The magistrate is not by vertue of his office to meddle with religion, or matters of conscience, to force and compell, men to this or that form of religion."[6] Staid, starched citizens of merry ole England could hardly believe their ears. The authorities were being challenged.

Baptists did more than merely talk; they acted. *Baptists broke laws.* Deliberately, premeditatively, with full awareness of what they were doing—Baptists broke laws. They broke laws in England and in America. They broke the laws because they felt them to be unjust laws. They broke them because they felt that there was a law that transcended civil law; it was the law of Scripture. So they refused to conform to civil statutes that curbed religious freedom.

Baptists paid for their protesting. No exaggeration, some bled. Some were publicly whipped. More than a few were imprisoned. All were buffeted with irrational name-calling. Society demanded order and obedience. Baptists responded that obedience is impossible and disorder inevitable when injustice prevails!

"Civil disobedience" was a popular phrase in America in the 1960s, but neither the term nor the idea is new. Our Baptist grandparents cut their teeth on it and survived by it. Leon McBeth, professor of church history at Southwestern Seminary in Fort Worth, Texas, was exactly right when he said that some contemporary Baptists would be "scandalized to learn *how* our Baptist ancestors expressed their dissent against the establishment."[7] Non-conformity, theological and political, has long been a part of the Baptist vocabulary.

II

The Lutherans have Martin Luther. Presbyterians have John Calvin. Methodists have John Wesley. But whom do Baptists have? Contrary to a popular belief, John the Baptist did not father us. We do not go back quite that far! Who then were our forebears? With what names do we personalize the Baptist heritage of nonconformity?

With John Smyth (Smith). As I said earlier, he is often called the first Baptist. Small wonder then that he was a religious refugee. Educated in the "liberal" tradition at Cambridge and an ordained Anglican, he proved himself a divisive man because of "personal preaching." This first Baptist-to-be was apparently socking it to persons of high places! So he lost his job! Wanting more fresh air for his soul than English atmosphere could provide, he scooted over to Holland. There he taught and preached what came to be known as basic Baptist distinctives.

John Smyth had a common name, but that was the only ordinary thing about him. "He was extremely sensitive to new light and singularly fearless in acting upon his convictions, and was, therefore, often in advance of his age."[8] He is reputed to be the first British person to plead for full liberty of conscience. Ralph Sockman once described Jesus as a "conservative revolutionary" who "knew that the suction of what is behind is a greater deterrent than the resistance of what is ahead."[9] John Smyth apparently knew that, too. He constantly tried to escape the "suction of what is behind." In doing so, he spearheaded the Baptist tradition.

A close associate of John Smyth in Holland was another English refugee by the name of Thomas Helwys. Convinced that it was his duty to return to England and minister to its citizens, and because of some disagreements with Smyth, Helwys made his way back to his native land and organized a church at Spitalfields in 1612. This is often called the first Baptist congregation on English soil. Helwys' return to his native country was an act of religious faith. It was also political rashness. He was imprisoned and may have died behind bars.

Helwys is credited with the first English publication demanding universal religious liberty. "Let them be heretics, Turks, Jews or whatsoever," said Helwys. "It appertains not to the earthly power to punish them in the least measure."[10]

The doctrine of full religious liberty, now so common and taken for granted, was then a perilous and fanatical concept. Helwys, a Baptist, was one of the leading fanatics.

III

One thing needs to be made clear about Smyth, Helwys, and others of their stripe. They did not buck the establishment—culture, society, church, and state—just for the sake of raw, red-blooded rebellion. Theirs was no adolescent kicking of the traces just to hear the clanging and clonging. They rebelled because they had a vision of something worth saving. They rebelled against the concept of a "parish" church because they believed the idea of a "gathered" church was worth saving. They rebelled against a state-enforced religion because they thought the freedom of the human spirit was worth saving. They rebelled against the priority of ecclesiastical institutionalism because they believed that the priority of the individual was worth saving.

C. S. Lewis described a character in one of his novels as having "a good deal of spaniel in him." Then Lewis added, "He liked to be liked." One cannot read Baptist history without feeling that early Baptists wanted to be liked. They certainly did not "like to be disliked." They started their denominational life with more maturity than that. But neither did Baptists "like to be liked" enough to muffle conscience and repress dissent. They therefore risked the agony of controversy and change.

"My! My! My! The more things change, the more Baptists remain the same." I thought in the historical half of my mind: "Hasn't always been so!"

Notes

[1]Gordon Kingsley, "Opposition to Early Baptists," *Baptist History and Heritage* (January 1969): 19.

[2]Daniel Featley, *The Dippers Dipt* (London, 1645) as quoted in ibid., 26.

[3]John W. Gardner, *Self-Renewal: The Individual and the Innovative Society* (New York: Harper & Row, 1963) 49.

[4]W. T. Whitley, *A History of British Baptists* (London: Charles Griffin & Co., Ltd., 1923) 4.

[5]For further reading on early Baptist theology, see Earnest A. Payne, *The Fellowship of Believers: Baptist Thought and Practice Yesterday and Today*; H. Wheeler Robinson, *The Life and Faith of the Baptists*; and Winthrop S. Hudson, ed., *Baptist Concepts of the Church*.

[6]As quoted in H. Wheeler Robinson, *The Life and Faith of the Baptists* (London: Kingsgate Press, 1946) 124.

[7]Leon McBeth, "Do Baptists Deserve a History?" *Home Missions* (January 1970): 14.

[8]A. C. Underwood, *A History of the English Baptists* (London: Carey Kingsgate Press Ltd., 1947) 44, 45.

[9]Ralph W. Sockman, *The Paradoxes of Jesus* (New York: Abingdon Press, 1936) 50.

[10]As quoted in Underwood, 47.

Chapter 1

The
"When Did Baptists Begin?"
Controversy
or
Baptists Argue about
Their History

I do not know of a Southern Baptist church anywhere that has had an acute attack of enthusiasm about Baptist history. Do you? Take your church, for example. When was the last time you had some dry-as-dust speaker describe all the roots and branches of your denominational family tree? Announce a seminar on Baptist history, and you have a mass exodus of church members looking for something "relevant" and "exciting."

"Let bygones be bygones" is the attitude of most Baptists toward their history. That attitude is o.k., except for the impossibility of it. Bygones are not *just* bygones. Our bygones are not has-beens. They are still with us, helping and shortchanging us, damning and redeeming us, perverting and saving us. Bygones are present. They are present whether you know it or not, whether you care or not.

I

Baptists have not always—usually, but not always—ignored their past. In fact, one of the best brotherly blood-lettings Southern Baptists ever had was about Baptist history. By "best" blood-letting I mean Baptists got hot! I do not mean that it was good, though some good flowed from it. By "brotherly" blood-letting I mean Southern Baptists fought each other.

This fraternal fight over Baptist history is popularly called "the Whitsitt Controversy." Dr. W. H. Whitsitt, president and professor of Southern Baptist Theological Seminary in Louisville, Kentucky, was one of the charter members of that exclusive Southern Baptist group known as "The Friendless Fraternity of Exiled Professors." The tension got so tight that somebody had to go. Poor Professor Whitsitt! He was in the wrong place saying the right thing at the wrong time. It was his turn to exit. He waved goodbye to Southern Seminary in 1899.

It is said that today one of the first so-called rules of life for faculty members on large university campuses is "Publish or Perish!" For Dr. Whitsitt the slogan turned out to be "Publish *and* Perish!" Dr. Whitsitt published some articles and a book entitled *A Question in Baptist History* and he perished from Southern Seminary. Before he left, however, his writings created one of the most bitter and divisive controversies in all of Southern Baptist history.

What did Whitsitt say that stirred up such a hornets' nest? Why all the fuss? Several issues were involved, but the basic issue was an argument over the age of Baptists. Whitsitt crossed swords with a prevailing interpretation of Baptist history that said that Baptists had lived in unbroken succession since New Testament times. The overwhelming opinion among Baptist historians today is that Whitsitt waved the "sharpest" sword. Whitsitt was right, but dull swords can cause bleeding, too. Whitsitt bled, but won. Later historical investigations have supported his point of view. Contemporary Baptist historians in the six Southern Baptist theological seminaries continue to teach Whitsitt's point of view.

Whitsitt's point of view—what was it? He said that Baptists began in 1641 when they "recovered" the practice of believer's baptism by immersion in England, and that it is historically inaccurate to trace the Baptist denomination back beyond that date. W. Morgan Patterson, a present-day church historian at Southern Seminary, said that Whitsitt "arrived at these conclusions after a thorough sifting of the primary sources and through the application of critical methodology."[1] That is one way of saying that Whitsitt had done his homework!

The historical error that Whitsitt wanted to correct was firmly entrenched in Southern Baptist life. Most Baptists in the latter half of the nineteenth century merely assumed that Baptists began in the year A.D. 30 and continued in unbroken succession. This successionist concept of Baptist history constitutes one of those ideas that enhances the position of a people and therefore goes unquestioned and unchallenged. The idea became a kind of Baptist sacred cow that one would touch or criticize at his peril. Successionism was too good not to be true, reasoned most Baptists.

The "Father of Baptist Church Succession" was an English Baptist minister by the name of G. H. Orchard. In 1823 he found himself in conversation with an Independent minister who maintained that Baptists were of recent historical origin. No historian, Orchard nevertheless refused to believe the minister and affirmed his confidence in the idea that Baptists had experienced a continuous existence "from the days of John the Baptists [sic], until now. . . ."[2] Immediately Orchard set out to prove his point by a study of church history.

Orchard was a perfect example of the fact that history can be terribly abused. As with the Bible, you can find what you want to find in history. Most religious denominations have! Orchard found what he was looking for by tracing the Baptist denomination back to the New Testament through all of the dissenting movements in Christian history. In other words, most of those groups that dissented from Roman Catholicism were "Baptists," according to Orchard. (One contemporary Baptist writer aptly but facetiously dubbed this "the mole-hole theory of succession, linking us to Jerusalem, Jesus, and John the Baptist in unbroken continuity, sometimes underground."[3]) The sad truth, however, is that some of those groups were less orthodox doctrinally than were the Roman Catholics. For the successionist, the sadder truth is that whatever and whoever the dissenting sects were, they were not the forerunners to modern Baptists.

The popularizer of Baptist successionism in America was J. R. Graves, who may have had more lasting influence on Southern Baptists than any other single individual in our 125-year history. Graves died in 1893, but before his death he saw Baptist Church Succession enthroned by most Southern Baptists as unquestionable orthodoxy. It was the only "right" thing to believe! So when the Whitsitt Controversy raged during the years 1896–1899, Dr. Whitsitt often fell heir to the odious label of a "heretic." A person's view of Baptist history had become a doctrinal issue of prime importance.

You can understand the ready acceptance given to the Orchard-Graves propaganda, if you are aware of what was going on in American religious life at that time. The nineteenth century was a time of keen denominational rivalry. Most denominations in the twentieth century merely think they are God's best; but in the nineteenth century they thought they were the only ones God had. Someone recently reported seeing a church billboard that announced: "This is the only church authorized by God to represent Jesus Christ in the world." This was the prevailing notion among some denominations in the past century.

> We are the choice elected few,
> Let all the rest be damned;
> There's room enough in heaven for you,
> But we won't have heaven crammed!

Public religious debates were hallmarks of the time. Great crowds would gather to hear hours of tedious theological nit-picking. Baptists versus Methodists, Baptists versus Church of Christ, and so on. Denominational life in the nineteenth century was marked by a zealous search for authority. Religious groups were going through what psychologists might call an "identity crisis." They were trying to establish themselves, to secure some solid justification for their existence. Historians refer to this search as a "High Church" movement and point to the Roman Catholic Church, the Anglican Church, the Campbellites, the Lutherans, and the Baptists as evidence.

As each denomination sought to prove its claim as the "true New Testament Church," Baptist Church Successionism proved to be a handy bit of ammunition for Baptists. "Why," claimed the Baptists, "we began with John the Baptist, have continued in unbroken succession ever since, and we can prove it." To prove that you are the oldest is to prove that you are the "onliest"—or so thought some Baptists in the 1800s.

II

Whitsitt challenged the prevailing idea of successionism—discreetly at first. Realizing the potential explosiveness of what Whitsitt wrote, one can understand why the professor first stated his thesis in anonymous magazine articles! (Date those articles 1880. Fifteen more years passed before the public knew who wrote them.) In 1893 Whitsitt published a similar article in *Johnson's Universal Encyclopedia*, but this time he signed his name. The war was on!

One inflamed soul wrote a letter to the *Western Recorder*, the Kentucky Baptist state paper, and asked:

> What did Dr. Whitsitt mean by writing that and publishing it in an Encyclopedia? What are the Trustees of the Seminary going to do about it? Does the *Recorder* agree with him?

The tone of the editorial response was an omen of things to come:

> The Recorder very emphatically does not agree with Dr. Whitsitt. We
> believe—past all conviction to the contrary—that the Baptists adopted
> immersion in the year 30, and have been immersing ever since.[4]

The person who led the "loyal opposition" to Whitsitt was Dr. T. T.
Eaton, editor of the Kentucky paper.

Other state papers took up the fight against Whitsitt. Associations and
state conventions passed resolutions asking for Whitsitt's historical hide.
He was charged with cowardice for not signing the earlier articles, with
dishonesty for not finding in historical research what Baptists had always
found, and with infidelity for not believing as a Baptist. As in every controversy when people take the reins off their emotions, misinterpretation
and misunderstanding resulted. Some of his opponents thought Whitsitt
was saying that Baptists "invented" baptism by immersion in the seventeenth century. He never intended to say that the immersion of believers
began at that time. He believed that idea came from the first century and
the New Testament. He was raising a question regarding the antiquity of
Baptists as a denomination and not baptism by immersion as a New Testament concept.

Friends are for tough times. Dr. Whitsitt had friends. One was Dr.
John R. Sampey, a fellow faculty member of Whitsitt. At the 1896 meeting of the Baptist association in Louisville, Kentucky, Sampey "secured
the floor against a bedlam of voices and talked in a passionate manner
for over an hour on this issue. Boldly he defended Dr. Whitsitt's integrity, scholarly competence, and Baptist orthodoxy."[5] As a matter of fact,
this Bible scholar, who taught Old Testament at Southern Seminary for
sixty years, must have gotten rip-roaring mad because he apologized to
the association the next day.

The Kentucky Baptist paper described Sampey's apology as follows:

> Dr. Sampey again took the floor to shake hands with the moderator and
> to say four things: "I do not believe," said he, "I will ever inflict a
> speech on Long Run Association as long as that one I dumped on you
> yesterday. In the second place, I do not believe I will make any such
> wild gestures and jump over the pulpit as I did yesterday. Thirdly,
> Brother Moderator, I do not believe I will ever get half as 'mad' as I
> was yesterday. And in the fourth place, I hope, in the goodness of God,

nobody will ever stir me up to get as mad as I was yesterday." This closed the episode.[6]

The faculty members at the Seminary unanimously adopted a statement in support of their president. They appealed to Southern Baptists "to stand by us, as we stand by our honored President, and to continue to give the institution your fervent prayers, your liberal support, your undiminished confidence."[7] They defended Whitsitt's scholarly competence, his scriptural soundness, and his denominational loyalty.

In spite of the faculty appeal and the tireless efforts of others to calm the waters, the situation got worse. Look at this resolution passed at the Kentucky Baptist State Convention of 1897!

> Resolved, that the Trustees of the Seminary from Kentucky be requested, and they are hereby requested, to urge, insist upon and vote for the retirement of Dr. Whitsitt from the Presidency of the institution and from the Chair of Church History.[8]

Four other state conventions—Louisiana, Arkansas, Texas, and Mississippi—followed the leadership of the Kentucky Convention.

More was to come. The place: Norfolk, Virginia. The date: May, 1898. The occasion: Meeting of the Southern Baptist Convention. The person: B. H. Carroll, prominent Baptist from Texas. The fly in the ointment: Carroll gave notice that he would make a motion at the 1899 meeting of the Southern Baptist Convention. The content of the motion: that the Southern Baptist Convention dissolve all relations with the Southern Baptist Theological Seminary.

The Kentucky Baptist Convention echoed B. H. Carroll one month later. Moreover, the Kentucky convention passed another resolution denying the seminary the right "to make any report nor present any appeals of any sort whatever to this body as long as Dr. Whitsitt shall be in any manner connected with the institution."[9]

Opponents of Whitsitt had played a trump card—financial withdrawal from the seminary. The choice was painful! The seminary loses either extensive financial support while Southern Baptists lose their only seminary, or a controversial history professor who just happened also to be president loses his job. Whitsitt made the choice for the seminary and for Southern Baptist theological education. He sent a telegram to the president of the seminary board of trustees. It was dated 13 July 1898: "I hereby resign my office as President of the Southern Baptist Theological Seminary and Professor of Church History to take effect at the close of the session of 1898–9." One sentence, brief but to the point. The ex-president later joined the faculty of the University of Richmond in Richmond, Virginia, and taught there until 1909.

Southern Baptist historians—the professional historians—were not through with it, however. They continued to teach what Whitsitt taught. Who said that times do not change? In 1969, seventy years after Whitsitt's resignation, a church history professor at Southern Baptist Theological Seminary, W. Morgan Patterson, wrote *Baptist Successionism: A Critical View*. Patterson candidly said, and obviously without fear of having to resign, that the concept of Baptist church successionism rests "on precarious historical and theological foundations."[10]

III

W. O. Carver, who studied under Whitsitt and later became a faculty member at Southern Baptist Theological Seminary, knew Whitsitt and the Whitsitt Controversy well. In a Founder's Day address at the seminary in 1954, Carver said that the election of Whitsitt as president of the seminary in 1896 "was the occasion for the most extensive, the bitterest, and in the issue the most decisive conflict ever to disturb the Baptists of America."[11] Maybe so. But what does the Whitsitt Controversy of the 1890s have to do with Baptists of today? Are the facts of the Whitsitt issue simply a collector's item that one approaches as an antiquarian, or do they touch contemporary Baptist life? They touch us.

The idea that Whitsitt was seeking to correct is very much alive to this very day. In the "Foreword" to his 1969 book, Morgan Patterson said, "The view of Baptist history examined here [successionism] is still widely held." Patterson even suspected that "it is probably the prevailing one among Baptists in the South."[12] You do not have to travel far in Southern Baptist life to find Baptist Church Successionism advocated, yet the idea lacks the passionate following that it enjoyed in the nineteenth century. Southern Baptists are learning gradually that successionism is neither historically demonstrable nor theologically necessary. We cannot prove it, nor do we need to do so. Valid church life is not based upon historical lineage but upon adherence to the Bible.

This controversy touches us at another point: Have you ever heard it said the "Baptists are not Protestants"? Do you know where such a statement originated? It came from the idea that Baptists existed *before* Protestantism emerged. It is a part of the successionist approach to Baptist history. Professional Baptist historians today claim that it is an idea without historical support, however. Like W. H. Whitsitt before them, these historians contend that Baptists originated out of English Protestantism. W. O. Carver told of visiting Whitsitt near the end of the latter's life. Carver said that the aging historian would always ask, "How are the Baptists getting on in Kentucky?" "Then," Carver said, "he would inquire especially about the 'Protestant Baptists.' "[13] Whitsitt spearheaded a tradition in Baptist life that said, "Baptists *are* Protestants."

Maybe the most important result to come out of the Whitsitt Controversy was that it awakened Baptists in general and Southern Baptists in particular to a sense of their history. To fight over your heritage is not a good way to learn about it; but even that is better than ignoring it altogether. The Whitsitt crisis stimulated an interest in the Baptist past. Baptists began to look over their shoulders to see where they had come from. That is always helpful.

Not only did the Whitsitt fuss stimulate interest in the history of Baptists but, as Carver said, Whitsitt

> aroused and promoted among Southern Baptists the concept and gradually and increasingly the study of their history *scientifically, objectively,* and in its wider historical context.

We have often gone to history to uncover evidence that would confirm our prejudices—denominational, theological, or national. But that is the manipulation of history, not the study of history. The study of history is a moral enterprise, moral in the sense that one must report honestly and fairly what is there.

Whitsitt was trying to be guided by his intellectual honesty rather than by his denomination's bias. He knew, however, that the scientific study of history was risky. He made an interesting entry in his diary on 27 February Thursday, 1890:

> I am casting about to begin writing a work on American Baptist history. It is an herculean task, and I must keep it all to myself . . . Baptist history is a department in which "the wise man concealeth knowledge." It

is likely I shall not be able to publish the work while I live, but I can write it out in full and make arrangements to publish it after my death, when I shall be out of reach of bigots and fools.

Whether or not Whitsitt ever wrote an exhaustive survey of Baptists in America, we are not sure. Of one thing we are sure: He did not keep his knowledge of Baptist history all to himself.[14]

Notes

[1]W. Morgan Patterson *Baptist Successionism: A Critical View* (Valley Forge PA: Judson Press, 1969) 28.

[2]As quoted in ibid., 25.

[3]Lewis E. Rhodes, "Southern Baptists Confronting the Challenge of a Disordered Society" in *Proceedings: 1968 Christian Citizenship Seminar on Christian Action in a Disordered Society* (Nashville: Christian Life Commission of the Southern Baptist Convention) 51.

[4]These quotes appear in John R. Sampey, *Memoirs of John R. Sampey* (Nashville: Broadman Press, 1959) 161.

[5]William A. Mueller, *A History of Southern Baptist Theological Seminary* (Nashville: Broadman Press, 1959) 81.

[6]Sampey, 85.

[7]As quoted in Sampey, 164.

[8]As quoted in Sampey, 87.

[9]As quoted in Frank M. Masters, *A History of Kentucky Baptists* (Middletown KY: Kentucky Baptist Historical Society, 1953) 416.

[10]Patterson, 6.

[11]W. O. Carver, "William Heth Whitsitt: The Seminary's Martyr," *The Review and Expositor* (October 1954): 464.

[12]Patterson, 5.

[13]Carver, 467.

[14]For a good and more extensive discussion of this controversy see James Thomas Meigs, "The Whitsitt Controversy," *The Quarterly Review* (January, February, March 1971): 41-61.

Chapter 2

The
"What about the Heathen?"
Controversy
or
Baptists Argue about Missions

We tend to forget. We tend to think that things have always been the way things are today. So, among other things, history is a "memory-jogger." It reminds us that the present is not the past, and often it makes us grateful that this is the case.

Baptists have not always been ardent advocates of missions—home or foreign. You may remember your preacher's illustration about William Carey, the father of modern missions, who stood up one day in a Baptist association in England and suggested that Baptists send missionaries to India. An older preacher barked at young Carey, "Sit down, young man. If God wants to save the heathen, He is God enough to do it without man's help." We tend to forget that.

At times Baptists have denounced missions, divided over missions, and, in some instances, destroyed missions. The speaker is inaccurate when he or she says, "Baptists have always been a great missionary people, born and bred in evangelistic fervor!" The speaker forgot his or her Baptist background. One wishes that person were right. If so, Baptists of America could have been spared one of their most damaging of all controversies, the so-called "Anti-Missions Controversy."

I

The Anti-Missions Controversy is an important chapter in Baptist life if one wants to understand contemporary attitudes of some Baptists regarding theology, worship, and support of the ministry, not to say anything concerning the missionary enterprise itself. If one ever wondered where Primitive Baptists came from or why some Baptists advocate missions but oppose mission boards, the anti-Missions Controversy will help answer some of the questions.

In the latter part of the 1700s, the American people began a jaunt westward that carried them over the mountains and onto the frontier of Tennessee and Kentucky. A number of Baptists made that trip. Between 1790–1810 one-fourth of the Baptists of Virginia were estimated to have migrated to Kentucky. During the same period, thousands of North Carolina Baptists spilled across the mountains to Tennessee. Baptists then scattered to other frontier and deep Southern regions.

Would the struggling Baptists make a go of it in their new wilderness? Absolutely! They transformed a religious jungle into a Baptist Zion. W. W. Sweet, a Methodist and one of the greatest of all American church historians, declared that no body of Christians was more suited for the frontier than were the Baptists. If you look at the figures, Sweet must have been right because Baptists experienced rapid growth beyond the mountains.

But one of our denominational ironies is just this: The frontier, an environment most conducive to the growth of Baptists, became the breeding ground and headquarters for the Anti-Missions movement among Baptists. The Anti-Missions Controversy rocked frontier Baptists from 1820 to 1840. This was prior to the organization of the Southern Baptist Convention, but the fact that Southern Baptists were without an institutional body does not mean that Baptists of the South escaped the results of the fierce missionary controversy.

Organized missionary activity among Baptists began on a nationwide scale in 1814. That was the year Luther Rice led in the formation of the Triennial Convention, a foreign missionary society that met once every three years. The thirty-three delegates who met in Philadelphia in May, 1814, had one primary purpose. They wanted to construct

> a plan for eliciting, combining, and directing the energies of the whole denomination in one sacred effort, for sending the glad tidings of salvation to the heathen.

The Convention appointed a Board of Foreign Missions to transact business while the Triennial Convention was not in session. (This was, I suppose, the first Executive Board!) The Board was to employ missionaries, make sure of their qualifications, appoint their field of labor, and fix the amount of financial compensation. Very professional and businesslike! Who could object to such a noble cause handled in such fine fashion? Baptists could! And plenty of Baptists did. The newly-formed organization became a primary target for the "anti" folk.

The Board of Foreign Missions appointed Luther Rice as "Agent." Rice traveled throughout the country rallying Baptists behind the missionary endeavor. Some he rallied; others he angered. Few were neutral. The missions movement was one of those "for" or "against" issues—no such thing as a "silent majority" or "silent minority."

Initially, Baptists of the West responded with some enthusiasm to the idea of missions. When Luther Rice visited Kentucky in 1815, he collected more money for missions than from any other state with the exception of Massachusetts. Most of the churches in Tennessee were friendly to the foreign missions cause, also. Rice was well received in the churches there and even secured the organization of a state foreign mission society.

The situation changed, however. In Tennessee missionary groups were broken up, and associations revoked pro-missions resolutions. Speaking of the anti-missionary sentiment, one contemporary said, "The current of prejudice had gradually swollen, until now no one cares to resist it."

Anti-missionism spread rapidly and extensively. No person ventured

> to open his mouth in favor of any benevolent enterprise or action. The missionary societies were dissolved, and the associations rescinded all their resolutions by which they were in any way connected with these measures.[1]

Within one decade, 1820–1830, the anti-mission movement threw Kentucky Baptists in chaos. Anti-mission forces in Mississippi destroyed the first statewide Baptist organization and nearly demolished the second, founded in 1836. Even in the Old Dominion of Virginia, twelve of thirty-four associations in 1845 were aggressively anti-mission. Look at the decline of missionary interest in Ohio! In 1820 Baptist churches of that region contributed $547.09 to missions, from 1821–1828 they gave zero, and in 1829 and 1830 the gifts were $10 and $5 respectively. Baptists of Alabama, Georgia, Missouri, Illinois, Indiana, and Louisiana were also affected. By 1846 there were 68,068 anti-mission Baptists in the United States; 45,000 of these were located in the frontier states.

II

What happened? Why the change of attitude regarding missions? It is an interesting story, and while the whole cannot be told here, enough can be said to identify the major forces at work in this crucial period of American Baptist history.

One of the major factors in the rise of anti-missionism was jealousy —*unredeemed ministerial jealousy!* The frontier Baptist preachers were generally uneducated, often downright illiterate. In 1817 the Triennial Convention began sending "home" missionaries to the frontier. John Mason Peck was the most famous of these missionaries. These preachers from the East were a more educated breed. While the typical frontier preacher was a farmer during the week and a preacher on Sundays, receiving his education mostly between the handles of a plow, the missionary preachers from the "urban East" had what the frontiersmen called "book larnin'." This threatened the grubby backwoodsmen.

One frontier preacher, whose personal jealousy had transformed itself into antagonism toward organized missions, is reported to have said: "We don't care anything about them missionaries that's gone amongst them heathens way off yonder." When pressed for reasons for his hostility, he admitted,

> Well, if you must know, . . . you know the big trees in the woods overshadow the little ones; and these missionaries will be all great, learned men, and the people will all go to hear them preach, and we shall all be put down. That's the objection.[2]

At least he was honest! But some things in life are tragic, even when we are honest about them. Jealousy is one of them!

From this jealousy of educated missionaries grew a suspicion of ministerial education in general. Baptists had not always scorned education. To the contrary, Baptists in Colonial America had put a high value on an educated clergy. Neither did all Baptists on the frontier view lightly the importance of an enlightened clergy. But amidst the deprivation and grubby individualism of the frontier, education was not considered a paramount factor in the life of a minister.

The primary issue was whether the preacher had received a call from God to the ministry. One anti-missionary association in Alabama summarized the frontier point of view:

> As to the education we know no objection, provided it is received *before* a call to the ministry, for Paul says, "Let every man abide in the same calling wherein he was called." . . . Oh, what an insult to Deity, that men should say that God has no power to qualify men for the ministry, after He has called them.

An anti-missionary preacher compared "theological schools to make preachers" to "the bottomless pit spoken of in Revelations. For a bottomless pit has no foundation in the Scriptures as an institution God."

"Highfalutin" language from the pulpit was not impressive. But a perspiring face, a passionate voice, and homespun illustrations were impressive. One person said that when pioneer preachers stood to preach "they usually threw the reins upon the neck of feeling and let her run full speed."[3] With their emphasis altogether on "heart" rather than "head," one can understand their fear of the educated Baptists from the East. It is altogether possible that some of the harsh feelings were elicited by the eastern preachers who paraded their learning.

Closely related to the ministerial jealousy between uneducated and educated was a sectional jealousy between East and West. Westerners saw Easterners as blue-blooded aristocrats. Easterners viewed Westerners as uncouth backwoodspeople. Compounding this geographical rivalry for Baptists was the fact that mission societies originated in the East, demanded a membership fee that was sometimes a considerable fee, and were controlled in the East. Given their previously established prejudices toward the East, frontier folk saw the missionary movement as an obvious nefarious plot whereby they were to be bilked for the benefit of money-mad citylickers. The pioneers bowed up at the smell of what John Taylor called "the New England Rat."

A second factor that aided the rise of anti-missionism was suspicion of missionary organizations. Frontier Baptists interpreted the increasing number of missionary societies as a trend toward centralization in church government and authority. Fearing that the independence of the local churches would be swallowed up in an eastern ecclesiastical superstructure, many churches and preachers lashed out at the missionary societies.

In his anti-mission pamphlet Daniel Parker noted that God did not send Jonah to Ninevah through a missionary society, nor was he

> sent to a seminary of learning to prepare him to preach to these Gen-
> tiles; but was under the tuition of a special order of God, and was in no
> case under the direction of any body of men whatever, neither did he
> look back to a society formed to raise money for his support.

The only organization the Bible knew was the church of Christ!

Baptists had always been rather protective of the freedom and authority of local church autonomy. The individualism of frontier living compounded this trend. When someone therefore began talking about a missionary society that had authority to send missionaries wherever it desired, many Baptists began to wonder if a conspiracy was at work against the local churches.

A third factor spurred on anti-missionism: money! The foreign missionaries such as Judson, the traveling agents such as Luther Rice, the home missionaries such as Peck, and the missionary societies such as the Triennial Convention wanted money! This sounded strange to a group that did not pay its own preachers, and frontier Baptists never became infatuated with that habit. As a matter of fact, many of the frontier preachers would have never thought of asking for money for themselves. Some frontier ministers thought it was unethical to receive pay for doing the Lord's work. God's gospel should be dispensed free of charge! One person said of the people of the frontier that they "loved the gospel, and they loved its ministers, but the soul of money drove all the good feelings from their heart."[4] A Baptist preacher contended that the Baptist doctrine concerning the ministry was: "The Lord keep thee humble, and we'll keep thee poor."[5]

Luther Rice visited the Elkhorn Baptist Association in Kentucky in 1815. Trying to fire the missionary imagination of the Kentucky Baptists, he was also seeking to secure their monetary support. One of the men who was later to become a leader in the Anti-Missions movement was "turned off" by Rice's appeal for money. He described Luther Rice's sermon with biting sarcasm:

> When Luther rose up, the assembly of thousands seemed strickened with his appearance. A tall, pale-looking, well-dressed young man, with all the solemn appearance of one who was engaged in the work of the Lord, and perhaps he thought he was. He spoke some handsome things about the kingdom of Christ; but every stroke he gave seemed to mean MONEY. He had the more pathos the nearer he came getting the money.[6]

For this anti-missionist, the entire missionary endeavor of the Triennial Convention was based upon the evil principles of "money and power."

Suspicion breeds distortion. Anti-missionists circulated stories saying that

> if the people went to hear a missionary they would be taxed and would be compelled to pay twenty-five cents for every sermon they heard, and every one baptized, there would be a tax of fifty cents to pay, and every year a tax of one dollar.

A classic case of misrepresentation growing out of the failure of conflicting parties to communicate!

Everything has to have a theology. There is a theology of sex, a theology of violence, a theology of ecology, and on and on and on. There was also a theology of anti-missions. Which comes first: theology or practice? Do we do a thing and then theologize it, or do we think a thing and then practice it? It is often impossible to tell. My guess is that in the case of the anti-missions controversy, theology probably came in second —to justify practice. At any rate, theology was also an important ingredient in the recipe for anti-missionism.

The theology of the anti-missions controversy was hyper-Calvinism, that old idea that a sovereign God does not need the help of finite humans to bring in the Kingdom of Heaven. Baptists viewed as gross heresy anything that smacked of the Methodist concept of salvation by works. "Election" and "predestination" were the "in" words of a person opposed to missions. "Converting the heathen is God's work," one would cry, "Let God do it!"

One association in Mississippi, denouncing the missionary program, clearly demonstrated the prevailing theology of the anti-missionists:

Surely you must have a great thirst for money that you should beg it in
the name of converting the heathen!—for if you know anything about
God, you know this, that it is His prerogative to convert the heathen, or
as many of them as he wants converted.

So were born the Primitive Baptists!

Daniel Parker, the father of a group of Baptists with the intriguing
name of the Two-Seed-in-the-Spirit Predestinarian Baptists, represented
the most extreme example of hyper-Calvinism. His theology was simple
and understandably anti-missionary. He said there were two seeds present
in the life stream of humanity, one good and the other evil. Every person
is born with one seed or the other, and nothing can be done about it.
Children born of the divine seed are children of God; children born of the
evil seed are children of the devil. Missions are superfluous, for people
cannot change what is already fixed and predestined. Parker's Two-Seed
group still exists—barely. In 1945 there were sixteen churches with a total membership of 201—but one would hardly expect great growth from
that kind of thinking.

Bad theology is a big obstacle. Needed change is often crippled by
wrong thinking. The missionary movement was retarded and, in some
areas, buried because of bad theology.

To summarize, here are four of the major factors in the rise of the
Anti-Missions Controversy: (1) the personal factor of ministerial jealousy,
(2) the organizational factor of fear of centralization, (3) the financial
factor of ministerial support, and (4) the theological factor of hyper-
Calvinism.

But there was a fifth factor without which the others would have
been impotent: the personnel of the Anti-Missions Controversy. A trio it
was: John Taylor, Alexander Campbell, and Daniel Parker. All were im-
placable and persuasive foes of Baptist missions. It just so happened that
they were also three of the most influential preachers on the frontier.

John Taylor fired the first significant shot. In 1819 he unleashed a
furious polemic with the bland title of *Thoughts on Missions.* Only the
title was bland, however, for Taylor referred to the missionary efforts as
the "New England rat." He said that the missionaries love money like a
horse-leech loves blood and budded Luther Rice "a modern Tetzel." (Tetzel, you may recall, was the Catholic priest who angered Martin Luther
by selling indulgences.) With age Taylor mellowed, and by the time of

his death he was living at peace with other missionaries. The old war-horse repented of his rampage, but not before inflicting untold harm on the organized missionary effort.

Daniel Parker died unrepentant. Neither age nor argument could tame his spirit. To his disciples, he was a Moses, a leader without peer. To missionary Baptists, he was "the notorious Daniel Parker." On one occasion Parker was at an associational meeting where Luther Rice preached and collected an offering for missions. Someone asked Elder Parker if he made a contribution. He answered, "No! He had no counterfeit half dollars; if he had he would have thrown in, but as he had none he would not throw away good money for such an object."

John Mason Peck described Parker as "one of those singular and extraordinary beings whom Divine Providence permits to arise as a scourge to his church." To be sure, Peck played ball for the opposite team, but without question Parker was born in the objective mood. His life, sermons, and writings reeked with negativism. He found his security in being against something. With intemperate zeal, he lashed out at the missions movement.

The last of the three fighters was Alexander Campbell, whose name is most commonly identified with the body of Christians known as the Disciples of Christ or the Churches of Christ. Campbell was a Baptist for a while, however, in fact, long enough to build up a massive following and lead thousands of Baptists out of the denomination.

The Baptists and the Campbelites divided because of several differences, including their understanding of baptism; but one of the basic problems was Campbell's attitude toward missionary organizations—unscriptural societies, as he called them. Like John Taylor, he later changed his mind on the questions of missionary societies, but after he had helped divide Baptists over the issue.

When the smoke had cleared from the Anti-Missions Controversy, Baptist ranks in the South were thinner. Yet, here may be an example of the oft-stated idea that quantitative decline does not mean a qualitative set-back. Pro-missionary Baptists came out of this abrasive conflict more committed than ever before to the idea of Christian missions.

Though they would engage in later arguments concerning the method of missions, whether through boards or local churches, most Southern Baptists came out of the anti-missions crisis firmly committed to some form of centralized missionary operations. At the same time that Southern

Baptists organized their Convention in 1845, they also established foreign and home mission boards.

The Anti-Missions Controversy also helped chart the theological course for future Southern Baptists. At least it ruled out one option: hyper-Calvinism. Missionary Baptists of the South continued to affirm the sovereignty of God in human history, but they refused to hide behind that idea when it undercut human responsibility. Southern Baptists came out of the missionary melee believing that humans are more than puppets.

Notes

[1] As quoted in A. H. Newman, *A History of the Baptist Churches in the United States* (New York: Christian Literature Company, 1894) 437, 438.

[2] As quoted in T. Scott Miyakawa, *Protestants and Pioneers* (Chicago: University of Chicago Press, 1964) 148.

[3] As quoted in Walter Brownlow Posey, *The Baptist Church in the Lower Mississippi Valley, 1776-1845* (University of Kentucky: University of Kentucky Press, 1957) 25.

[4] Ibid., 32.

[5] As quoted in ibid., 32.

[6] As quoted in Robert A. Baker, *A Baptist Source Book* (Nashville: Broadman Press, 1966) 80.

Chapter 3

The
"What about the Blacks?"
Controversy
or
Baptists Argue over
Slavery and Segregation

One would have to be a religious Rip Van Winkle to be unaware of the fact that Southern Baptists, among other American churchpeople, have been going through a revolution. When all of the rhetoric is silenced, one of the major reasons for the fuss is the question, "What about the blacks?" The quarrel is not a new one for Southern Baptists, however, nor has it been subdued.

Davis C. Woolley, the late Executive Secretary of the Historical Commission of the Southern Baptist Convention, wrote that the racial issue "is one of the most inflammatory subjects ever to be discussed in the Convention."[1] After scanning Southern Baptist history, one may think that Woolley grossly understated the case. It has not only been inflammatory; it has been explosive!

I

Like the English Baptists of the seventeenth century, the Southern Baptist Convention was born in the fire of controversy. What caused the fire? Was it theological in nature? Did Southern Baptists create their own convention because they feared theological liberalism among Baptists in the North? No, not really. When the delegates to the first Southern Baptist Convention gathered in Augusta, Georgia, in May, 1845, they were not protesting doctrinal heresy. Said those first Southern Baptists from Augusta,

> Let not the extent of this disunion be exaggerated. . . . Northern and Southern Baptists are still brethren. *They differ in no article of the faith.* They are guided by the same principles of gospel order. . . . We do not

regard the rupture as extending to foundation principles, nor can we think that the great body of our Northern brethren will so regard it.[2]

Theology was not the issue in Augusta. Not at all!

Nor was ecclesiology (the doctrine of the church) the primary issue at Augusta. One interpretation of the organization of the Southern Baptist Convention is that Baptists of the South wanted one type of denominational structure while those of the North wanted another. This idea has probably been given too much attention, however.

It is a fact that when Baptists of America formed their first national organization (the Triennial Convention) in 1814, there were differences of opinion regarding what type of organizational structure would be best. Some delegates wanted a very decentralized approach to denominational life. Others wanted a more centralized approach, which was more popular in the South. Decentralization eventually won out. Individual societies (such as Foreign Missions Society, Home Missions Society, etc.) were organized, rather than one denominational Convention.

When Southern Baptists met in 1845 to form a Southern Baptist organization, they constructed a more centralized denomination than Baptists in America had at that time. Some Southern leaders wanted the centralized approach all along. Now they had their opportunity. They would do it "their way."

One must insist, however, that the nature of the denominational organization was neither the occasion nor the underlying cause of the formation of the Southern Baptist Convention. One only has to read what Southern Baptists themselves said at their first meeting to know that this is true. Baptists in America would probably have never suffered denominational division over ecclesiology. It simply had not been that hot an issue among them. In Augusta ecclesiology was not the issue at stake.

A third issue, beyond theology and ecclesiology, possibly would have created organizational division among Baptists in America, though it was certainly not a major cause or immediate factor in the formation of the Southern Convention. This was the issue of home missions.

Baptists in America formed the American Baptist Home Missionary Society in 1832. Shortly after its formation, Baptists of the Deep South, Southwest, and West began to air objections. They felt that a disproportionate number of missionaries were sent into northern and eastern regions, to the sad neglect of their own territories. The Society, however, was not engaged in a deliberate policy to overlook the needs of these areas.[3]

Nonetheless, calls went out prior to 1845 for the organization of a new society that would better attend to the needs of the West, Southwest, and South. None of these calls bore permanent fruit. It is altogether possible, however, that this issue would have eventually separated Baptists in America. Had it done so, the Baptist division might have been more East-West than North-South, but home missions was not the primary concern of the persons who traveled to Augusta.

Well, let me finally answer the question. What was the issue, the major issue and the immediate issue, in the organization of the Southern Baptist Convention? It was slavery, the same issue that tore the innards out of the nation a few years later. A cultural earthquake struck this young nation during the years 1830–1865; but before the quake created a political chasm between North and South, it had sliced the churches down their Mason-Dixon Line.

The Southern Baptist Convention was organized in defense of the mid-nineteenth-century Southern culture. Lest you quickly and self-righteously blast the Baptists of 125 years ago and threaten to leave Southern Baptists to join a denomination unmarred by the scar of slavery, I must add another word. Baptists were not alone. The octopus of culture has little respect for denominational boundaries. It will choke the Christian ideals of a Presbyterian or a Methodist just as soon as it will a Baptist. Evidence: Methodists of the South formed their slavery-justifying denomination a few days before the Baptists, Presbyterians a few years later.

Churchgoers of the South had not always been unanimous in their justification of slavery, just as churchgoers of the North had not been unanimous in their condemnation of it. Baptists, North and South, denounced slavery in the 1700s and early 1800s. In 1790 some Virginia Baptists affirmed "that slavery is a violent deprivation of the rights of nature and inconsistent with a republic government." They suggested that Baptists "make use of every legal measure to extirpate the horrid evil from the land." In 1796 the Ketocton Association of Virginia declared that slavery was a transgression of the Divine Law. The Association also appointed a committee to draw up a suggested plan of general emancipation. Other associations in other states passed anti-slavery resolutions.

The Baptist voice against slavery was not loud; nor was it widespread or long in meeting stiff opposition. The Ketocton Association's plan of emancipation was indicative of the situation. According to a Virginia Baptist historian the association was "treading upon delicate ground." He went on to say that the emancipation plan

> excited considerable tumult in the churches, and accordingly in their letters to the next association they remonstrated so decidedly that the Association resolved to take no further steps in the business.[4]

As Baptist associations and committees encountered grassroot hostility, they backed off. They then began to say that slavery was an economic and civil issue and did not therefore properly belong in religious discussions. This rationale for evading the plight of the black person would long be a strategy in Baptist circles of the South.

From about 1790, Southern Baptists' attitudes regarding slavery stiffened. More and more, Baptists, with other Southerners, justified and defended slavery. What caused this stiffening of the Southerners?

For one thing, a revolution in Southern agriculture occurred. Whitney's cotton gin in 1792, plus other developments, made slavery more economically profitable. Slavery suffered less denunciation as cotton became king. Also, the growing spirit of Northern abolitionism played a role. A powerful sentiment for emancipation emerged in the North in the 1830s. Abolitionists eventually attacked more than the system of slavery; they scorned slaveholders too. Sectional polarization developed in a hurry. Southerners became defensive not only of their Christian character; they also defended slavery, often in the name of the gospel. Northerners became aggressive in the name of the same gospel.

II

As stated previously, the first national organization of Baptists was the Triennial Convention. Organized in 1814, its primary focus was foreign missions. By 1832 Baptists of America had formed a Home Missions Society. These two organizations became the focal point of the slave controversy for Baptists, North and South.

The Triennial Convention was experiencing agitation and division over the slavery issue as early as 1834. By 1840 militant Baptist abolitionists in the North had organized themselves into a Baptist Anti-Slavery Convention. They advocated immediate emancipation. They also became letter writers. In a letter to their Northern Baptist counterparts, who were more moderate on slavery, the abolitionists argued that all Northern Baptists were obligated to take action against Southern Baptists if slavery persisted. To Southern Baptists, they said

> Southern churches were urged to confess the sinfulness of holding slaves, to remonstrate against civil laws which entrenched the system, and if these plans were disregarded, to gather their families and possessions and emigrate to the North.[5]

Baptists of the South were not tickled with the contents of that letter.

The issue was surfacing: Should slaveholders be allowed fellowship in the Triennial Convention? More specifically, should a slaveholder be appointed a missionary by the Convention? Times of tension often present moderates with the leadership. Such was the case here—for a few years. The moderates of the North and the pro-slavery Southerners joined forces to guarantee the peace and future of the Triennial Convention.

This uneasy alliance could prop up the Convention only for a while. After three or four years, the Triennial Convention, like Humpty Dumpty, would have a great fall. (As it turned out, all of the Baptists in the United States have not been able to put the Convention back together again.) Before the collapse, however, moderate Northerners and pro-slavery Southerners convinced the Triennial Convention to take a position of "neutrality" on the slave issue.

At the 1844 meeting in Philadelphia, the Triennial Convention reaffirmed a position of neutrality. This was a position taken several times before, based upon the fact that the Triennial Convention had only one purpose: foreign missions. Members of the Convention could speak as individuals on the slave question, but no one could speak *in* the Convention or *for* the Convention on this divisive issue.

Harmony within the Convention took priority over stand-taking on slavery. Southerners thought they had the victory, but constant and forceful pressure was exerted on the Northern Baptists to disassociate themselves from the evil of slavery. Neutrality was impossible forever. During the Protestant Reformation, burly and impulsive Martin Luther once said of Erasmus, his cautious humanist friend, "He wants to walk on eggs without breaking them." The Triennial Convention tried that for awhile, but a showdown was inevitable.

Baptists of Alabama were not convinced that the Triennial Convention was really neutral on the issue. They had reason for suspicion.[6] On 25 November 1844, Baptists of that state addressed a fateful letter to the Board of Managers of the Triennial Convention. Consisting of a Preamble and six Resolutions, the letter called for candor from the Northern leaders. The essence of the letter is found in the second resolution. It is important enough to quote in full:

> Resolved, that our duty requires us, at this crisis, to demand from the proper authorities in all those bodies to whose funds we have contributed, or with whom we have in any way been connected, the distinct, explicit avowal that slaveholders are eligible, and entitled, equally with non-slaveholders, to all the privileges and immunities of their several unions; and especially to receive any agency mission, or other appointment, which may fall in the scope of their operations or duties.

School was out! It was a time for candor. The Board of the Triennial Convention issued a stinging reply: "If . . . any one should offer himself as a missionary, having slaves, and should insist on retaining them as his property, we could not appoint him." That was candor! But just to be sure to avoid ambiguity they continued: "One thing is certain; we can never be a party to any arrangement which would imply approbation of slavery."

Alabama Baptists had also threatened to withdraw financial support. The paraphrased response of the Northerners could be stated as "Take your money and blow." Southern Baptists could take a hint. They blew— to Augusta.

Virginia Baptists considered the action of the Board of the Triennial Convention "an outrage" on Southern rights. They argued that the Board had pulled off an unlawful and unconstitutional act. Technically, that was true. For the Constitution of the Triennial Convention, framed by slaveholders and non-slaveholders alike, did not address itself to slavery. Moreover, the 1844 Triennial Convention had approved a resolution that chased the slave issue out of the Convention with a declaration of "neutrality."

The Board's anti-slavery statement was dubbed "a flagrant breach of trust." The Virginia Baptist Foreign Mission Society said, "To remain united with the Board is impossible. Self-respect forbids it." Subsequently, they adopted and circulated the following resolution that resulted in the organization of the Southern Baptist Convention:

> Resolved . . . that in the present exigency, it is important that those brethren who are aggrieved by the recent decision of the Board in Boston, should hold a Convention, to confer on the best means of promoting the Foreign Mission cause, and other interests of the Baptist denomination in the South.

Augusta, Georgia was suggested as the place for the Convention and 8 May 1845, the date. Southern Baptists heeded both suggestions.

A few voices among Southern Baptists discouraged the idea of a new Convention. For example, the Tennessee Baptist Foreign Mission Society, while believing the board of the Triennial Convention had violated a trust and "rendered themselves justly obnoxious to the censure of the whole church," nevertheless advised against the proposed new Convention. The Tennessee Society believed the Triennial Convention, in its next general meeting, would have reversed the decision of the Board. But Baptists of the South did not plan to wait two years to find out.

Two hundred ninety-three "delegates," representing such diverse Baptist bodies as local churches, ministers' conferences, associations, state conventions, educational institutions, and missionary societies, met in Augusta and voted to organize a new Convention. They indicated that the division was "painful" but necessary because "our brethren have pressed upon every inch of our privileges and our sacred rights."

The purpose of the Convention, according to Article II of the Constitution, was "to promote Foreign and Domestic Missions, and other important objects connected with the Redeemer's kingdom." In the public statement that Southern Baptists sent out, a paragraph depicted not only the purpose of the Convention but also the basic rationale toward slavery.

> Our objects, then, are the extension of the Messiah's kingdom, and the glory of God. Not disunion with any of his people; not the upholding of any form of human policy or civil rights; but God's glory, and Messiah's increasing reign; in the promotion of which, we find no necessity for relinquishing any of our civil rights. We will never interfere with *what is Caesar's*. We will not compromise what is God's.[7]

What was the meaning of "what is Caesar's" that was placed in italics? Slavery, obviously. The pattern established by early Baptist associations and continued awhile by the Triennial Convention of dodging the slave issue by declaring it beyond the religious domain persisted.

III

Augusta didn't settle the problems. Southern Baptists were not finished with the question, "What about the blacks?"

From slavery, Southern Baptists eventually turned to debate racial prejudice and its social manifestation: segregation. This time the disagreement did not involve Northern and Southern Baptists. The argument was among Southern Baptists. There was no organizational division, but fiery debate abounded.

The year 1954 was a pivotal one for race relations in America. In that year the Supreme Court of the United States issued its landmark decision on public school segregation. At its annual convention of the same year, the Southern Baptist Convention adopted a report of their Christian Life Commission that acknowledged that the Court decision "is in harmony with the constitutional guarantee of equal freedom to all citizens, and with the Christian principles of equal justice and love for all men." The adopted report also commended the Supreme Court for deferring the application of school desegregation, urged Baptists to conduct themselves in the spirit of Christ in the period of adjustment, affirmed a belief in the public school system of America, and advised Christian statesmen and leaders to use their leadership positions to avert new and bitter prejudices.

Southern Baptists had spoken as a Convention to the issue of race relations before 1954. One may find resolutions and recommendations regarding race in the Convention proceedings of 1939, 1940, and 1941. According to T. B. Maston (who, more than any other person, has scrutinized the subject of Southern Baptists and race relations), Southern Baptists took their most significant convention action in 1947. That year messengers to the Convention adopted a special report that said many good things such as, "We shall think of the Negro as a person and treat him accordingly;" "We shall continually strive as individuals to conquer all prejudice"; "We shall teach our children that prejudice is un-Christian," etc.[8]

Individual Southern Baptists had also spoken out on the race issue. While Hitler and his crusade of anti-Semitism hovered over Europe and the world of 1942, one Baptist editor wrote,

> Until we break down racial prejudices within the boundaries of our own land and prove by its working that a program of racial adjustment is practical, we shall be heard with little serious attention when we speak about removing the larger and far more complicated racial antipathies and antagonism which the would-be dictators of the world are using today for their own advancements.[9]

Notice two things about Southern Baptists and race prior to 1954. One, most of their public pronouncements came through Convention resolutions. It has always been much easier to adopt a resolution in a convention than to implement it in a local church. Every pastor knows that. Secondly, the resolutions that Baptists were adopting had to do with racial prejudice in a general sense. Few addressed themselves to the question of integration.

Following the Supreme Court decision of 1954, the racial situation in the South became most intense. The emerging civil rights revolution angered many Southern whites, many of whom were Baptists. Desegregation came gradually. When Baptist students at Ridgecrest Assembly requested in 1946 that Negro Baptist students be represented at the next annual encampment, the petition was first refused. The policy of segregation at Baptist assemblies was later changed. Southern Baptist seminaries did not officially desegregate until 1951, while Wayland Baptist College in Texas became the first white Baptist college in the South to enroll a Negro in the same year. Today, most Baptist institutions are integrated.

Integrating denominational institutions was much easier than integrating local churches. In 1968 the Home Mission Board of the Convention conducted a study that indicated 510 churches had black members; 3,724 other churches expressed a willingness to receive Negro members. Both of those figures have increased since 1968.

Desegregation has come gradually, painfully, and certainly not without controversy among Southern Baptists. Churches were divided, pastors dismissed, and editors rebuked. In 1968 the Southern Baptist Convention, meeting in Houston, Texas, engaged in a spirited controversy over the adoption of a document called "A Statement Concerning the Crisis in Our Nation." Among many other things, the statement said, "We will personally accept every Christian as a brother beloved in the Lord and welcome to the fellowship of faith and worship every person irrespective of race or class."[10] Before the statement was adopted by a vote of 5,687 (72.85%) to 2,119 (27.15%), an attempt had been made to table the main motion. Once again, however, this was a public statement made by a convention. Action was left to individuals and local churches.

According to volume 3 of the *Encyclopedia of Southern Baptists*, in 1971 there were at least four predominately white congregations in the Southern Baptist Convention who had Negro pastors. To be sure, a very small number—but that is a long, long way from May, 1845, in Augusta, Georgia. Some Southern Baptists might agree today with the words of T. B. Maston, written in 1967: "Progress has been made and is being made, but when we compare what we have done with what we should have done it seems mighty little."[11] It is an old, nagging, controversial question for Southern Baptists, and it keeps coming up: "What about the blacks?"

Notes

[1]Davis C. Woolley, "Major Convention Crises over a Century and a Quarter," *Review and Expositor* (Spring 1970): 80.

[2]*Proceedings of the Southern Baptist Convention, 1845*, 17. (Italics mine.)

[3]See Robert A. Baker, *Relations Between Northern and Southern Baptists*, (Fort Worth TX: the author, 1948) 27-39.

[4]Robert B. Semple, *A History of the Rise and Progress of the Baptists in Virginia*, rev. G. W. Beale (Richmond VA: Pitt and Dickinson, 1894) 392.

[5]Baker, 50.

[6]The Home Mission Society had recently refused to appoint a slaveholder as a missionary. The slaveholder had been suggested by Georgia Baptists, but Georgia Baptists also made it clear that this was a "test case." The candidate was turned down, so the Mission Society said, not because he was a slaveholder, but because he represented a "test case." Southerners were enraged. It was this event that aroused Alabama Baptists to write the Board of Managers of the Triennial Convention.

[7]Most of the documents pertaining to the formation of the Southern Baptist Convention may be seen in these sources: *Proceedings of the Southern Baptist Convention, 1845*; Robert A. Baker, *A Baptist Source Book with Particular Reference to Southern Baptists* (Nashville: Broadman Press, 1966); *The Quarterly Review*, vol. 30, no. 1, 2.

[8]*Southern Baptist Convention Annual*, 1947, 47-48.

[9]As quoted in Kenneth K. Bailey, "Southern Baptists, 1940-1963," *Baptist History and Heritage* (January 1968): 20.

[10]*Southern Baptist Convention Annual*, 1968, 68.

[11]T. B. Maston, "Southern Baptists and the Negro," *Baptist Student* (May 1967): 28.

Chapter 4

The
"What about Other Denominations?"
Controversy
or
Baptists Argue about
The Church

The following incidents are true. I know; they happened to me! Names have been deleted, not in order to protect the innocent, but because I cannot remember all of the names. The incidents come out of twelve years of pastoral experience in Baptist churches.

Incident One

When I was a seminary student at New Orleans, I became pastor of a rural church in southeast Louisiana. About two weeks after I went to the church a lady of the community, whom I thought was a member of the church, came to my house wanting to talk. Here was her problem: She and her husband had recently moved into the community after living most of their lives in Chicago, San Diego, Brooklyn, and other such "foreign" regions. Both the Mr. and the Mrs. were Baptists, but they were American Baptists (Northern) and not Southern Baptists. She had been reluctant to join the rural church in southeast Louisiana because she had heard that she might have to be re-baptized. She asked, "Do Southern Baptists not accept baptism from Baptist churches of other Conventions? That's what I've heard." I answered, "There is some truth to what you heard. A few Southern Baptists might have reservations about your baptism."

Incident Two

After a worship service one night a young ex-Quaker-lady-recently-turned-Baptist walked up to me and said, "They told me the other night in Training Union that Baptists aren't Protestants; where in the world did they get such an idea?" I cannot tell you all that I told her, but a part of the answer is found in chapter 2 of this book, and a little more of the answer is found in this chapter.

Incident Three

I was speaking at a Presbyterian youth retreat on the subject, "Who are the Baptists?" After I had worked hard for twenty minutes painting Baptists as a loving, tolerant, open group of twentieth-century Christians, a teenager blurted out, "Why won't you Baptists let us Presbyterians take the Lord's Supper with you?" I explained that some Baptists would welcome her to the Lord's Table. I did not, however, bother to explain why some Baptists would frown on "open communion." That is part of what this chapter is about.

Incident Four

"Is it true," asked a Methodist man, "that Southern Baptists won't accept my baptism even though I was immersed as an adult?"

Incident Five

"Why is it," asked an Episcopalian collegian, "that Southern Baptists don't participate in more interdenominational activities? Do you folks think you are the only true church?"

★ ★ ★

End of incidents. But *why* have some Baptists demanded other Baptists to be rebaptized? *Where* did Southern Baptists get the notion that Baptists are not Protestants? *Why* have some Baptists made "a thing" out of limiting the Lord's Supper to Baptists? *Why* do most Baptist churches reject "alien immersion," or immersion performed by other denominations? *Why* have Baptists been shy about interdenominational activities?

Well, as in most cases, the answer is complex. Many factors and ideas shape denominational life. If one understands a movement known as Landmarkism, he or she can better interpret the above incidents.

I

Landmarkism developed among Baptists in America in the 1850s, and its influence is still felt to this very day. A basic idea of Landmarkism is "the sole validity of Baptist churches."[1] In other words, *Baptist churches are the only real Christian churches!* Church historians refer to such a movement as "high churchism"; sociologists would dub it "exclusivistic"; and ordinary churchpeople, reared in the twentieth century, would probably write it off as "denominational arrogance." Call it what you will; it is one of the facts of Baptist history.

The Landmark movement exerted some influence on Baptists of the North. Its greatest foothold, however, was among Southern Baptists. While the excessively rigid attitude of the movement is dead or dying (few, if any, Southern Baptists maintain today that Baptist churches are the *only* true churches), vestiges of Landmarkism continue to crop up in Southern Baptist life.

There were three primary leaders in the rise of Landmarkism. They have often been spoken of as "The Great Triumvirate." The father and popularizer of the movement was J. R. Graves (1820–1893). Originally from Vermont, Graves finally settled in Nashville, Tennessee, in 1845, about two months after the formation of the Southern Baptist Convention. He became a member of the First Baptist Church in Nashville, where he eventually was embroiled in a controversy with the pastor, R. B. C. Howell. In 1846 Graves became assistant editor and in 1848 editor of *Tennessee Baptist,* a post he held until his death in 1893.

Graves was a pastor, evangelist, editor, author, publisher, denominational leader, but most of all a controversalist! Possessed with an overdose of charisma and locomotive energy, he drove himself tirelessly. As his son-in-law and biographer said, "There was no still life in him. He had no idea of resting like the lark in the soft dawn of morning."[2]

J. R. Graves was a Baptist come to do battle. His first sermon, preached in Jessamine County, Kentucky, was an omen. His text was, "Adam, where art thou?" and in it he gutted the religious chameleons, those void of fixed religious principles, those too timid to announce and defend their faith. He was not the kind to compromise when he was convinced, and he was never unconvinced. "When he unsheathed his sword he threw the scabbard away," said his admiring son-in-law, but many of his fiercest opponents would have quickly agreed with that assessment. After reading him—and reading about him—he was the kind of guy you wish you could have known personally, so that your love could be more legitimate or your disapproval more passionate.

Through his efforts and influence, Graves spread Landmarkism rapidly and extensively among Baptists in the South and Southwest. The author of the article on J. R. Graves in the *Encyclopedia of Southern Baptists* said, "He influenced Southern Baptist life of the nineteenth century in more ways, and probably to a greater degree, than any other person." Many Southern Baptist historians agree.

Dr. J. M. Pendleton was the second most important personality in the Landmark movement. A pastor and professor, Pendleton was the theologian of Landmarkism. In 1852 Pendleton, pastor of the Baptist church in Bowling Green, Kentucky, invited J. R. Graves to preach a revival meeting in the church. After Graves arrived in Bowling Green and discovered that Pendleton was in the habit of receiving "alien immersion" as valid baptism, he almost returned to Nashville. Pendleton prevailed upon him to stay.

During the revival the evangelist must have come down hard on the issue of baptism—denouncing both "alien immersion" and infant baptism—because "there was considerable excitement among Pedobaptists (infant-baptizers) on the subject of baptism, and several sermons were afterward preached by Methodist and Presbyterian ministers."[3] Seventy-five people were converted in that revival. And while the pastor was not numbered among those seventy-five, he had been converted—to J. R. Graves' thinking. The paragraph below, taken from Pendleton's autobiography, reflects not only the growing relationship between the two men, but also the origin of the term "Landmark."

From the time of the meeting . . . , I became a regular contributor to the *Tennessee Baptist*, a weekly sheet published in Nashville, J. R. Graves, editor. I wrote on various subjects and was requested to write several articles on this question: "Ought Baptists to Recognize Pedobaptist Preachers as Gospel Ministers?" I answered in the negative and wrote four articles which were afterward published in pamphlet form under the title, "An Old Landmark Re-set." Bro. Graves furnished the title, for he said the "Old Landmark once stood, but had fallen, and needed to be re-set." So much for the name.[4]

The little tract, "An Old Landmark Re-set," written by Pendleton and named and published by Graves in 1854, revealed the Baptist exclusivism that characterized Landmarkism. In his later years J. M. Pendleton refused to subscribe to some of the more extreme and dogmatic aspects of Landmarkism. But he helped to get the movement airborne. He could be heard saying near the end of his life, "Baptists can never protest effectually against the errors of Pedobaptists which the preachers of the latter are recognized as gospel ministers. This to me is very plain."[5]

A. C. Dayton (1813–1865) was the third party in the Triumvirate. Converted from Presbyterian to Baptist views in 1852, Dayton joined forces with Graves and assumed a writing ministry. He is remembered primarily as the author of a religious novel, *Theodosia Ernest*, that depicts the true church and is, of course, Baptist.

With less powerful personalities at the helm, Landmark ideas would have never gained the prominence they enjoyed. But these were strong, colorful people with a sense of mission and deep convictions. They crusaded to see their ideas accepted. J. R. Graves boasted in 1880 that only one out of sixteen Baptist newspapers in the South rejected the basic tenets of Landmarkism. To say the least, Graves and his cohorts had been influential.

How or why did Landmarkism get such a firm toehold in Southern Baptist life? First, some of the emphases that the Landmark movement organized into such a tightly knit system antedate Landmarkism in Baptist life. Some of the Landmark teachings were not so much "innovations" as they were "intensifications" of Baptist ideas. Landmarkers perverted Baptist history via exaggeration. They affirmed that Baptists had always been Landmarkers. As Baptist historians and theologians know, this was patently not the case.

Second, Landmarkism emerged in the context of some bitter denominational rivalries. These were the days of denominational debating, especially between Baptists and Methodists and Baptists and the followers of Alexander Campbell. J. R. Graves endeared himself to a number of his fellow Baptists early in his ministry as a great apologist for the denomination. They therefore followed him through the years.

Third, Landmarkism had a means of popularizing itself—through a Baptist newspaper of which Graves was editor. For some years following 1869, the *Tennessee Baptist* served as the official paper for Arkansas, Louisiana, and Mississippi, as well as for Tennessee. Graves had the media; he also had the market. Fourth, Graves was a capable person who persuaded others by his tremendous dedication to what he taught. The movement cannot be understood, in terms of its teaching or growth, apart from the man.

II

Earlier I said that Landmarkism was a "tightly knit system"—very tightly knitted. Ecclesiology, the doctrine of the church, was its consuming concern. What was the essence of the Landmark system? *The primacy of the local church.* "Church" to a Landmarker meant a local and visible and completely independent congregation of baptized (immersed) believers that could trace its history back to the time of Christ. Only Baptist churches were true churches. Organizations practicing non-Baptist ideas did not, therefore, fit into the category of a "true" church. Because non-Baptist organizations were not "true churches," only "religious societies," they had no authority to authorize a person to preach. Nor were their ordinances valid. With all of this being true, as Landmarkers contended, what should be the Baptist attitude toward other denominations?

As a distinct movement within the Baptist tradition, Landmarkism began in 1851 at Cotton Grove, Tennessee. J. R. Graves submitted a series of five questions, later to be known as the "Cotton Grove Resolutions," that constituted the first official pronouncement of the Landmark movement.

To let you taste the flavor of Landmarkism, the "resolutions" are printed below. You will doubtless be able to tell that Graves answered all of the questions, with the exception of number four, with a resounding "no."

> 1st. Can Baptists consistently, with their principles or the scriptures, recognize those societies, not organized according to the pattern of the Jerusalem church, but possessing a different *government*, different *officers*, a different class of *membership*, different *ordinances, doctrines* and *practices*, as the Church of Christ?

2nd. Ought they to be called Gospel Churches or Churches in a religious sense?

3rd. Can we consistently recognize the ministers of such irregular and unscriptural bodies as gospel ministers in their official capacity?

4th. Is it not virtually recognizing them as official ministers to invite them into our pulpits or by any other act that would or could be construed into such a recognition?

5th. Can we consistently address as brethren, those professing Christianity, who not only have not the doctrines of Christ and walk not according to his commandments, but are arrayed in direct and bitter opposition to them?[6]

In essence, these resolutions disavowed the authority of non-Baptist churches, ministers, and ordinances. The conclusions of the Cotton Grove Resolutions were clear to all: only Baptist churches are gospel churches! Graves labeled all other churches and denominations as "religious societies."

Three years after the Cotton Grove meeting, J. M. Pendleton's famous essay, "An Old Landmark Re-set" hit the Landmark press. The next year, in 1855, the term "Landmark" was used for the first time on the floor of the Southern Baptist Convention. In that year the messengers to the Convention debated the propriety of permitting ministers from other denominations to "be invited to seats in the Convention, to aid by counsel and advice."

Heretofore, this had not been an issue in the Southern Baptist Convention. Davis C. Woolley was right on target in saying, "These discussions related to the 'true church' and her ministers. This subject was at the heart of J. R. Graves' 'Old Landmark' doctrines."[7]

In 1880 J. R. Graves wrote the definitive work on his movement. It was entitled *Old Landmarkism: What Is It?* One of his major purposes in writing the book, he said, was

> to establish the fact in the minds of all, who will give me an impartial hearing, that baptist churches are the churches of Christ, and that they *alone* hold, and have alone ever held, and preserved the doctrine of the gospel in all ages since the ascension of Christ.[8]

Care should be taken in defining Landmarkism. Graves did not deny that there were Christians outside Baptist churches, even though his

earlier statements such as the fifth Cotton Grove resolution came dangerously close to such an idea. For Graves the issue was "the true church,"
not spiritual regeneration. He believed that one must be a Christian before joining the true church ("Blood Before Water," he often said), and
therefore there could be Christians outside the church. Debating a Methodist on one occasion, Graves said, "I wish one thing to be distinctly
understood, i.e., the question is not whether the individual members of
the Methodist Society here are *Christians* or not."[9] Graves claimed he
was "unchurching" religious organizations, not "unchristianizing" the
members of those organizations.

III

Landmark doctrines had some very practical implications for Baptist life.
The first of these is seen in the extreme emphasis upon the local church.
Baptists prior to Landmarkism, both in England and America, had always
stressed the independence of local Baptist churches. Landmarkers took
this perfectly legitimate Baptist concept, blew it all out of proportion, and
came dangerously close to making a fetish out of it. This is one example
of the perversion via exaggeration I referred to earlier.

Among other things, this meant that Landmarkism became gravely
suspicious of all ecclesiastical boards beyond the local church level.
Agencies that sought to coordinate the activities and ministries of the
many individual Baptist churches came under suspicion. Mission boards
and their authority for supervising missionary activities, for example,
were eventually rejected by the more radical Landmarkers. They contended that only local churches had scriptural authority to examine, appoint,
and supervise missionaries.

Landmark opposition to the "board method" of missions expressed
itself on three distinct occasions in the Southern Baptist Convention.[10]
The first was in 1859 at the meeting of the Southern Baptist Convention
in Richmond, Virginia. Several months before the Convention, J. R.
Graves declared that "no man has lower views of the authority of a Missionary Board . . . than we have." He thought the audacity of the Foreign
Board to examine the religious experience of prospective missionaries
was "a high-handed act."

A compromise resolution settled the issue in 1859, with the Foreign
Mission Board left intact. But the anti-conventionism and anti-boardism

of Landmarkism re-surfaced between 1885–1893 in a movement known as "Gospel Missionism." Several factors converged to form Gospel Missionism, but ideologically the movement continued the Landmark opposition against mission boards. Once again, however, the missionary methods of the Southern Baptist Convention survived.

Finally, and inevitably, the split came. A new Baptist denomination was born out of protest. Those whose emphasis on the local church excluded cooperation through Convention-wide boards organized the Baptist General Association in Texarkana, Arkansas. Ben Bogard, the leader of the newly formed group, once wrote concerning "the thirteen evils of conventionism." His considered conclusion was, "A Convention is unknown to the Scriptures . . . and should not be tolerated by the churches."[11]

Bogard's group was thoroughly Landmarkist. Not only in their sentiment of anti-boardism but also in their Baptist exclusivism, they continued the emphasis of J. R. Graves. One of their early leaders wrote, "Why, it is patent as the day that the only true churches of Jesus Christ in the world today are landmark Baptist churches."[12]

The Landmark Baptists continue to the present. In 1924 the name was changed from the Baptist General Association to the American Baptist Association. What was the effect of the Landmark attack on the missionary operations? Some think Southern Baptists came out of the fray more committed than ever before to their missionary methodology. With the exit of the Landmarkers, Southern Baptists were unified in their approach to doing missions.

Organization of a distinct Landmark denomination did not mean the total elimination of Landmark influence on the Southern Baptist Convention, however. In his emphasis upon the church as being local, Graves also insisted that the church was totally visible. This concept was in contrast to the idea of an "invisible" or "universal" church which would include more than a local congregation of believers.

J. M. Pendleton disagreed with Graves at this point. Also, most Baptist theology prior to Graves had little trouble defining the church as both local and universal, visible and invisible. Nevertheless, Graves' concept of the church found an audience among many Southern Baptists. It is interesting to note that when the Southern Baptist Convention approved a Confession of Faith in 1963, the only debate came on one sentence: "The New Testament speaks also of the church as the body of Christ which includes all of the redeemed of all ages." The statement was adopted, however.

Landmarkism, with its emphasis on the local and visible nature of the church, continued to affect Baptists of the South. A second characteristic of Landmarkism was its peculiar interpretation of Baptist history. Claiming that Jesus established a visible kingdom, that *true* churches constitute that kingdom, and that the kingdom has always existed (because Jesus said it would never perish), Graves logically concluded that the *true* churches have had an unbroken historical succession leading back to New Testament times. Remember, *true* churches are *Baptist* churches!

You can understand why this idea has been named the "Jerusalem-Jordan-John" theory of Baptist beginnings. If one accepts this view, you also understand why that person insists that Baptists are not Protestants. Baptists, unlike Protestants, it is argued, did not "protest" against the Roman Catholic Church and form a new church. Baptists, according to this view, pre-date the Protestant Reformation and Roman Catholicism. You also recognize this to be the theory of Baptist history that W. H. Whitsitt opposed. The Whitsitt controversy, discussed in chapter one, is an outgrowth of Landmarkism.

A third inevitable result of Landmark teachings was that some Baptists hardened their attitude toward ministers of other denominations. The "Cotton Grove Resolutions" and Pendleton's important tract, "An Old Landmark Re-set," were both concerned with the belief that Baptists should not acknowledge ministers of other denominations as "official" gospel ministers. Specifically, and practically, this meant that Baptists should not invite non-Baptist ministers to preach in Baptist pulpits, and baptism, even if immersion, is not legitimate if performed by a non-Baptist minister.

The Landmark Baptists who formed their own denomination in 1905 have perpetuated the policy of isolationism toward other denominations. Within the Southern Baptist Convention this reserve toward other religious groups has also been present, though not as extreme. Landmarkism is not the only explanation for this reservation among Southern Baptists, but it certainly is an important influence.

The fourth area where Landmarkism helped shape Southern Baptist ideas has to do with the ordinances. As indicated earlier, Landmarkers rejected "alien immersion" because it was performed in a non-Baptist church by a non-Baptist minister. "Alien immersion" was also rejected because of what Landmarkers called its irregular "design" or purpose. This was especially true in relation to the Church of Christ, which taught that baptism was a necessary step in salvation.

Even before the rise of Landmarkism, Baptists were divided over the validity of "alien immersion." However, there was no unanimity on the matter. The error of Landmarkism was in distorting Baptist history and claiming that all Baptists once denounced alien immersion.

Southern Baptists still debate the validity of "alien immersion." What about it? Should a person who has been immersed in the name of the Trinity as a believing adult in a Methodist Church be accepted by a Baptist church? Or should the Baptists "re-baptize" that person? One of Southern Baptists' most informed students of Baptist history said,

> To be consistent with the heritage of Baptists, the judgment of the validity of non-Baptist baptism should be made by each congregation, and that without censure from fellow Baptists.[13]

The Lord's Supper is another area where a trace of Landmarkism may be seen in some Southern Baptist churches. Reasoning that only Baptist baptism is valid baptism and that baptism is a prerequisite to the Lord's Table, Landmarkers followed the policy often described as "closed communion" or "strict communion." As with alien immersion, closed communion has, at times, been a hotly debated issue in Baptist history. English Baptists, in particular, can supply "big" Baptist names to support either side of the issue. Charles Spurgeon, for example, practiced "open communion" in his church.

In America, however, Baptists have been more uniform in their practice. Here "the almost unanimous practice of Baptists has been closed communion."[14] Graves went further than to deny the Lord's Supper to people of other denominations. He said that only members of the local Baptist church administering the supper partake of communion. A Baptist could not take communion in any but his or her local church! This type of restricted communion was not followed by all of Graves' followers, nor has it influenced Southern Baptist practice to any great extent. Many Southern Baptist churches continue to practice "closed communion" with regard to other denominations. On the other hand, a number of Southern Baptist churches gladly welcome all Christians to the Lord's Table.

There is no single Southern Baptist "position" on the issue. In 1966 at the Southern Baptist Convention in Detroit, a messenger from an Arkansas church protested the seating of messengers from the First Baptist Church, Russellville, Arkansas, and moved that they be denied official seats in the Convention because the church had adopted a doctrinal statement advocating the practice of open communion and the acceptance of alien immersion.

Wayne Dehoney, President of the Convention, ruled the motion out of order and gave three reasons for his ruling: (1) The Constitution of the Southern Baptist Convention does not make these two matters a condition for seating messengers in the Convention; (2) the "Baptist Faith and Message" adopted in 1963 does not declare a position on these matters; and (3) traditionally and historically the Convention has never made these matters a test of fellowship. The Convention accepted Dehoney's ruling without objection.[15]

To some degree, one could say that the ghost of J. R. Graves was at that Convention—and he was ruled out of order! Without question, Landmarkism is one of the most significant developments in the life of Baptists in America.

Notes

[1]Hugh Wamble, "Landmarkism: Doctrinaire Ecclesiology among Baptists," *Church History* (December 1964): 429.

[2]O. L. Hailey, *J. R. Graves: Life, Times and Teachings* (Nashville: Broadman Press) 44.

[3]J. M. Pendleton, *Reminiscences of a Long Life* (Louisville KY: Press Baptist Book Concern, 1891) 103.

[4]Ibid., 103, 104.

[5]Ibid., 105.

[6]As quoted in William Wright Barnes, *The Southern Baptist Convention, 1845–1953* (Nashville: Broadman Press, 1954) 104.

[7]Davis C. Woolley, "Major Convention Crises Over a Century and a Quarter," *Review and Expositor* (Spring 1970): 167. See John A. Broadus, *Memoir of James Pettigrew Boyce* (New York: A. C. Armstrong & Son, 1893) 98-99.

[8]As quoted in Robert A. Baker, *A Baptist Source Book with Particular Reference to Southern Baptists* (Nashville: Broadman Press, 1966) 142.

[9]*The Graves-Ditzler Debate* (Memphis: Southern Baptist Publication Society, 1876) 927. See also *Old Landmarkism: What Is It?* in Baker, 144.

[10]See the excellent summary article, David L. Saunders, "The Relation of Landmarkism to Mission Methods," *The Quarterly Review*, vol. 26, no. 2 (1966): 43-57.

[11]See ibid., 56.

[12]As quoted by John E. Steely, "The Landmark Movement in the Southern Baptist Convention," in Duke K. McCall, ed., *What Is the Church?* (Nashville: Broadman Press, 1958) 142.

[13]W. Morgan Patterson, "The Role of Baptism in Baptist History," *Review and Expositor* (Winter 1968): 39.

[14]W. Morgan Patterson, "The Lord's Supper in Baptist History," *Review and Expositor* (Winter 1969): 32.

[15]*Southern Baptist Convention Annual*, 1966, 47.

Chapter 5

The
"What Must Baptists Believe?"
Controversy
or
Baptists Argue about Theology

"The world broke in two in 1922 or thereabouts," said Willa Cather. It did not, literally, but the world in general, and America in particular, was certainly busy trying to plug the holes created by the gushing currents of change. It really looked like everything nailed down was coming loose.

Life had not been the same since the middle of the nineteenth century, and it would never be the same. Immigration had changed America's religion: from "Protestant Empire" to religious pluralism. Industrialization changed America's vocation: from farmer to factory hand. Urbanization changed America's home: from pasture to pavement.

By 1922—to use the novelist's date again—nothing had undergone the challenge of change as much as the ideas by which people lived. There had been intellectual revolution afoot! Freud challenged a person's way of relating to self; Marx, the way of relating to others; and Darwin, the way of relating to nature.

With change comes controversy. This is an inexorable law of human history. The church, as all other institutions of society, eyeballed change. For some persons, it was "love at first sight." Willing to marry the present and forget the past, they became known as "Modernists." For others, it was cautious flirtation. They liked some of what they saw in change, but the past was still attractive, too. You can label them "Conservatives" or "progressive Conservatives" or "Conservative Modernists," depending where you want your emphasis. For still others, change was viewed not as a lover but a bandit, trying to steal what was lovely and fundamental in life. So you can call these persons "Fundamentalists." These are general and dangerous terms because, as someone said, they can too easily degenerate from labels into libels; but they give us a starting point.

Is there any wonder, then, that in the 1920s American Protestantism experienced what church historians now call the Fundamentalist-Modernist controversy? In a real sense in which many American churches "broke in two" during this controversy. "1922 or thereabouts" is as good a date as any, if you just have to have a date.[1]

I

Baptists were not exempt from the combat. In the late nineteenth and early twentieth centuries, they were racked by theological fist-fights. This was true of English Baptists, American (Northern) Baptists, Canadian Baptists, and Southern Baptists. Each of these groups had its own unique controversy, but underneath much of the yelling and name-calling were two basic issues: scientific evolution and biblical interpretation.

While our primary concern here is with Southern Baptists, one can better interpret and appreciate their conflict in the context of the battles of their denominational kinsmen. The English Baptist argument is known as "The Downgrade Controversy." Principal antagonists were two of the tallest spirits British Baptists have ever produced: Charles Haddon Spurgeon vs. John Clifford.

Spurgeon, who once bragged of smoking cigars to the glory of God, was one of the greatest preachers ever to mount a Christian platform. One minister described him as "the sauciest dog that ever barked in a pulpit." His sermons are still read—and preached! Clifford, a great preacher in his own right, was known primarily for his denominational statesmanship and leadership in social reform. He was the first president of the Baptist World Alliance. Both Spurgeon and Clifford were warm spirited and devout Christian men.

Charles Spurgeon suspected heresy of creeping into Baptist ranks, and he accused certain unnamed pastors of initiating "a new religion which was no more Christianity than chalk was cheese." He called for Baptists to adopt a written creed to protect the denomination. British Baptists rejected his plea for a binding doctrinal statement, accepted his resignation from the British Baptist Union in 1887, and expressed disapproval of his issuing general accusations without spelling out the alleged heretics.

Believing firmly in the inspiration and authority of the Bible but never wanting to repress the freedom to reinterpret the Bible, Clifford led the resistance to Spurgeon. The Downgrade Controversy is representative of a number of honest Baptist struggles. Spurgeon wanted orthodoxy, even if it meant restriction of some freedom of thought. Clifford wanted liberty, even if it meant the presence of what some believed to be unorthodox teaching.

Writing a half century after the controversy, one British historian said, "After more than fifty years, few, if any, Baptists are now other than thankful that the Union took the stand it did and refused Spurgeon's demand that it should accept a definite creed in place of its Declaration of Faith."[2] While British Baptists refused Spurgeon at this one point, they did not forget him or fail to enshrine him in their history. A life-size bronze statue of the great preacher was placed in the denominational headquarters.

English church members were in fraternal combat in the last part of the nineteenth century, but the Fundamentalist-Modernist battle brewing in North America made the English conflict look like a Sunday afternoon picnic. Wayne E. Ward defined Fundamentalism as "an ultraconservative theological movement, and sometimes a reactionary religious attitude, which has cut across many denominations and affected all parts of Christendom."[3] Fundamentalism's arch-enemy was Modernism. Denying biblical literalism, biblical inerrancy, and biblical infallibility, Modernism wanted to reformulate traditional theological concepts and make them more amenable to the modern scientific mind. This could be done, they contended, without sacrificing the religious truth of the Christian faith.

Fundamentalism, like Modernism, was a theological centipede. It had many different branches, so any attempt at generalizing gets you into historically muddy water. Three events in Fundamentalism help cast light on the movement. First, between the years of 1910 and 1912, a series of twelve small paperback volumes entitled *The Fundamentals: A Testimony to the Truth* was published. Financed by two wealthy California laymen, this set was to be sent free of charge to "every pastor, evangelist, missionary, theological student, Sunday School superintendent, Y.M.C.A. and Y.W.C.A. secretary in the English speaking world."[4] Eventually around three million copies were printed. In his book on *The History of Fundamentalism*, Stewart G. Cole said that in the publication of these books "the historian finds the clear emergence of fundamentalism."

The Fundamentals stressed what has often been called the Five Points of Fundamentalism. While these Five Points constitute a gross oversimplification of the movement, they do point to the common beliefs of fundamentalists. The Five Points were : (1) divinely inspired and inerrant Scriptures, (2) deity of Christ and virgin birth, (3) the substitutionary atonement, (4) Christ's bodily resurrection, and (5) His personal, premillennial, and imminent second coming. Writing articles in *The Fundamentals* were at least three Southern Baptists: J. J. Reeve and Charles B. Williams of Southwestern Seminary in Forth Worth and E. Y. Mullins, president of Southern Baptist Theological Seminary in Louisville, Kentucky.

A second important event that helped solidify the Fundamentalism movement was the formation in 1919 of the World's Christian Fundamentals Association. Over 6,500 leaders gathered in Philadelphia to launch an effort to save American churches from the menace of Modernism and especially from the evolutionary concepts of Charles Darwin. Northern Baptists, Canadian Baptists, and Southern Baptists eventually provided strong leaders for the Association.

Without a doubt the most memorable religious event in America in the 1920s was the Scopes Monkey Trial held in 1925 in the sleepy little town of Dayton, Tennessee. It was the third event that highlighted the religious conflict of the era. John Thomas Scopes, a high school coach and substitute biology teacher, was accused and tried for violating the state's recently enacted anti-evolution law that prohibited the teaching of the scientific theory in the classroom.

The trial pitted William Jennings Bryan, prosecutor and Presbyterian Fundamentalist, against Clarence Darrow, defense attorney and agnostic. Dayton virtually became a three-ring circus. In fact, there were enough dramatics present in the trial to make it a Broadway play, *Inherit the Wind*, and later a movie by the same name.

Between 1921 and 1927, thirty-seven anti-evolution measures were introduced in twenty state legislatures. Only five won approval. These were in Tennessee, Oklahoma, Florida, Mississippi, and Arkansas. The battle of evolution—fought in legislatures, courts, and public schools—was also fought in the churches of America. The relationship between religion and science and the corollary issue of biblical authority posed the battleground.

This was the background for the conflict among Baptists in North America. Canadian Baptists and Northern Baptists were more directly affected, in terms of denominational division, than were Southern Baptists.

Among Canadian Baptists, the Fundamentalist movement was spearheaded by T. T. Shields, pastor of the Jarvis Street Church in Toronto, and directed primarily against alleged Modernism at McMaster University, the Baptist owned school. By the end of 1927, the Ontario-Quebec Baptist Convention had excluded Jarvis Street church from the denomination. Shields then organized the Union of Regular Baptist Churches. Baptists in Central Canada have been divided ever since.[5]

Baptists in the Northern United States also divided during the Fundamentalist-Modernist controversy. W. B. Riley, pastor of First Baptist Church in Minneapolis, led the fight for Fundamentalism; while the most renowned "Modernist" was Harry Emerson Fosdick, once described as "the Jesse James of the theological world."

Northern Baptist Fundamentalists made several efforts to restrain what was considered destructive theological tendencies. First, they demanded that Northern Baptist colleges and seminaries be investigated for Modernist teachings. The investigation was made and the schools exonerated in 1921. Second, in 1922 Riley tried to persuade the Northern Baptist Convention to adopt a confession of faith to insure doctrinal uniformity. In the place of a clear-cut doctrinal statement, however, Northern Baptists adopted a resolution stating "that the New Testament is the all sufficient ground of our faith and practice, and we need no other."[6] When a third effort failed, directed this time against the Foreign Missionary Society, some of the more conservative Northern Baptists withdrew to form a new Baptist body.

II

Modernism never strutted in the South as it had in the North. For Southern Baptists, this meant that the Fundamentalist-Modernist controversy was not as grave an issue as it had been among Northern Baptists. But there was tension, and there would be separation, but it would be small.

Numbered among those Southern Baptists who could be called leading Fundamentalists were such people as T. T. Martin of Mississippi, C. P. Stealey of Oklahoma, and John W. Porter of Kentucky. Concerned primarily with what they considered Modernist teachings, and especially evolution, they took constant pot-shots at Baptist schools and professors.

While these men spelled trouble for the harmony of the Southern Baptist Convention, Southern Baptists had one Fundamentalist among them who—in terms of sensational tactics, vituperative rhetoric, and pulpit dramatics—possessed no rival, North or South. He was J. Frank Norris, pastor of the First Baptist Church of Fort Worth, Texas.

Before the civil courts of Texas, Norris was indicted for arson, tried for perjury, and acquitted on a murder charge! The state Baptist Convention of Texas censored him in 1922, refused a seat to a delegate from his church in 1923, and expelled him and his church from the Texas Convention in 1924. He was a forceful, dynamic preacher and a rare bird who loved to fly in the fires of controversy.

J. Frank Norris became pastor of First Church in Fort Worth in 1909 and remained there until his death in 1952. When he was called to the Fort Worth pastorate, only one family voted against him out of the three hundred and thirty-four people who voted. The deacon who voted "no" explained his vote before the church:

> I am not opposed to J. Frank Norris; I am for him, but this church is in no condition for his type of ministry. If he comes, there will be the all-firedest explosion ever witnessed in any church. We are at peace with the world, the flesh, the devil, and with one another. And this fellow carries a broad axe and not a pearl handled pen-knife. I just want to warn you.[7]

"This fellow carries a broad axe!" How absolutely apt for J. Frank Norris!

He carried "a broad axe" within his local church fellowship. While the church had serious internal strife and overt division, the congregation also knew phenomenal growth. From a membership of 900 in 1911, by 1928 the church increased to 12,000 members, with 5,200 average attendance in Sunday School. Most of the growth of the church has been attributed to the individual sensationalism of Norris.

He carried "a broad axe" to city hall, accusing political officials of corruption, graft, and immorality. Dr. Norris preached a sermon on July 11, 1926, in which he described the mayor of Fort Worth and his associates as a "two by four, simian-headed, sawdust-brained, bunch of grafters." He accused his enemies of "tampering with the wires" of his radio station and declared that "some of you low down devils that monkey around this property, arrange for your undertaker before you come around here." To an applauding congregation he announced that his guards would "shoot to kill."[8]

The next Saturday a friend of the mayor's, a lumberman by the name of D. C. Chipps, entered the pastor's study and an argument followed. Two hours later newspaper boys peddled extra editions of their papers with headlines reading: "D. E. Chipps, Lumberman, Slain by J. Frank Norris." That was 17 July 1926. The next January the pastor was acquitted in a Texas court on the grounds of self-defense.

Norris also carried "a broad axe" into denominational struggles. In October, 1921, a Fort Worth newspaper carried this terse advertisement: "Sunday night Dr. Norris will expose infidelity in Baylor University." The next Sunday night he gave the Baptist school in Waco a thorough tongue-lashing.

> With a flowing tide of words, with violent gestures and the poise of righteous indignation, he proceeded to cry that compromise, modernism, complacency, and infidelity were undermining the fortress of the Baptist faith in the South—Baylor University at Waco.[9]

Through his newspaper, *The Searchlight*, the fiery preacher continued to focus on Baylor University. Norris was especially concerned about a sociology professor whose book, according to Norris, advocated evolution and rejected inspiration of Scripture. In 1921 the Texas Baptist Convention appointed a committee to investigate the charges against Baylor. Norris lost his battle as Baylor was given the approval of the state Convention. Nonetheless, by 1923 Professor Dow had departed from Baylor.

Norris kept fighting Baylor and his denomination in general. In 1923 he said,

> I intend to start a fight on evolution and on the denomination and I never expect to stop until it is extracted, root and branch, and if the denomination is split, it will split over the question of evolution.[10]

But by this time Norris had already run into the ire of his denominational family. His local Baptist association excluded his church in 1922, primarily for his censoriousness and non-cooperation.

He was having a running battle with several of the most respected men among Texas Baptists: George W. Truett of First Baptist Church in Dallas; J. M. Dawson, pastor of First Church in Waco; and L. R. Scarborough, president of Southwestern Seminary. Dr. Scarborough would eventually write a stinging little tract entitled "The Fruits of Norrism."

Scarborough called "Norrism" "an old cult under a new name," and among several other demonic characteristics said

> it thrives on sensationalism, misrepresentation and false accusations of good men and true causes. It masquerades under the cloak of anti-evolution, anti-modernism, anti-catholicism in order to ride into public favor and cast poisonous suspicion on the leadership of constructive Christianity.[11]

The Baptists were battling!

If Norris had problems finding acceptance among leading Southern Baptists, he did not lack for friends in Fundamentalist circles beyond his denomination. Especially had Norris come to know and admire the work of T. T. Shields and W. B. Riley. The admiration was mutual. The three of them constituted a Baptist Fundamentalist triumvirate in North America: Shields in Canada, Riley among Northern Baptists, and Norris in the South.

Together they led in the formation of the World's Christian Fundamentals Association in 1919. In 1922 Shields, Norris, and Riley issued a "Call and Manifesto" to the Baptist clergy of Canada and the United States. In response to the call the Baptist Bible Union of North America was organized in May, 1923, at Kansas City. The purpose of the union was "to give the people the fullest information respecting the ravages of Modernism in all departments of . . . denominational life."[12]

Thus, a Pan-Baptist Fundamentalist organization for North America was born. It was strong and vocal, harassing all major Baptist denominations until about 1927. By 1930 the original organization had died.

III

With persons like Norris firmly committed to purging Southern Baptists of heresy, and with the agitation that came from organizations such as the Baptist Bible Union of North America, and with the widespread caution on the part of moderates concerning the new scientific theories, it was inevitable that the issues ultimately would appear on the floor of the Southern Baptist Convention. They did.

One has difficulty describing the conflict of the 1920s among Southern Baptists as the Fundamentalist-Modernist Controversy. Apparently, there were few, if any, confirmed Modernists among Southern Baptists. Some were open to the new science, but the vast majority of Southern Baptists accepted the theology of Fundamentalism. They were reluctant to accept the constant carping and effort at denominational domination by the more radical Fundamentalists, however.

Nevertheless, throughout the 1920s, the Southern Baptist Convention, in formal sessions, addressed itself to the relationship of science and religion. When the Convention met in 1922 at Jacksonville, Florida, the committee reporting for the Education Board issued two cautions to Southern Baptists. First, the committee warned that "great care should be exercised lest, by innuendo and nebulous criticism, the minds of the people be weaned away from loyalty to their schools" and "indiscriminate criticism is not the best way to correct an error in an individual or school." This was, obviously, a move to counter the attacks that were already being launched by persons like Norris.

"But this should not be the end of caution," the report continued. The education institutions of Southern Baptists were urged "not to use the textbooks in their curriculum which are calculated to undermine the faith of the students in the Bible." The profound conviction of the reporting committee was that one could not "understand the Bible and believe both the Bible and the accepted theory of evolution" as set forth in some science textbooks.

The 1922 messengers were further reminded of President E. Y. Mullins' annual sermon and the applause he received from the Convention when he said:

> We have been much concerned over modern rationalism and the false assumptions of materialistic science. . . . It seems to me three things are clear. First, we will not tolerate in our denominational schools any departure from the great fundamentals of the faith in the name of science falsely so-called. Second, we will not be unjust to our teachers, nor curtail unduly their God-given right to investigate truth in the realm of science. Firm faith and free research is our noble Baptist ideal. Third, we will be loyal to every fact which is established in any realm of research, just as we are loyal to the supreme fact of Christ, His virgin birth, His sinless life, His atoning death, His resurrection and present reign.

Obviously, President Mullins was trying to steer the Convention on a middle course as he described "firm faith and free research" as "our noble Baptist ideal."[13]

The next year, 1923, E. Y. Mullins entitled his presidential address to the Convention, "Present Dangers and Duties." He evidently hoped to calm the waters by speaking publicly to the issue once again. He reiterated the refrain of "free research" but protested against unestablished scientific theories parading as confirmed facts. Also, he echoed, in a more elaborate and arousing presentation, the emphasis on "a firm faith." After stating what he considered to be the basic "supernatural elements in the Christian religion," he said that adherence to these truths is "a necessary condition of service for teachers in our Baptist schools."

On the motion of a messenger from Oklahoma, that part of Dr. Mullins' address referring to "Science and Religion" was officially adopted as "the belief" of the Convention. But this did not go far enough for some of the radicalsJ. F. Brownlow of Tennessee offered a resolution calling for the appointment of a committee that would cooperate with the trustees of all Baptist colleges "in bringing about the death" of evolutionary teaching on Baptist campuses. The resolution was rejected "on the ground of interference beyond the province of the Convention." Colleges and universities owned by state Baptist conventions could not be supervised by the Southern Baptist Convention.[14]

By the time the convention met in Atlanta in 1924, the controversy had intensified. An effort was now being made by the more extreme Fundamentalists to pressure the Convention into accepting a binding doctrinal statement. Motions by C. P. Stealey and R. K. Maiden to this effect were, however, rejected by the Convention. In the name of peace-seeking, a special committee was appointed "to consider the advisability of issuing another statement of the Baptist faith and message." The committee, chaired by E. Y. Mullins, was to report to the 1925 Convention in Memphis.

Before the Convention met in Memphis, the Southern Baptist Educational Association, an organization of denominational educators, issued a statement cautioning church colleges to "avoid alliance with either Fundamentalism or Modernism." The Education Association also asserted that the "Bible cannot be taken literally and never was meant to be." In response, Mississippi Fundamentalist T. T. Martin proposed that the Southern Baptist Convention divide.

Let all who endorse . . . this stand taken by the Southern Baptist Educational Association go into one convention; let all who reject and repudiate this action go into the other convention." He warned if this were not done, "there is going to be fearful division and strife.[15]

Strife continued, but there was no "fearful division." The special committee presented its report to the Memphis Convention in 1925. The report consisted of a Confession of Faith (the Confession was a revision of the older New Hampshire Confession plus ten additional articles), a carefully worded preface on the meaning of confessions of faith, and a closing statement on "Science and religion" (this was a duplication of the Mullins statement adopted by the 1923 Convention).

Some individuals on the committee and others throughout the Convention obviously looked askance on the idea of a Confession of Faith, for the committee recommended the document with the qualifying words, "in the event a statement of the Baptist faith and message is deemed necessary at this time."

The Convention of 1925 deemed it necessary, because the Confession was adopted along with the rest of the committee's report. A part of that report, as mentioned above, was an introductory statement explaining the nature of Baptist confessions of faith. This Convention affirmed that the articles of the Confession were not "complete statements of our faith, having any quality of finality or infallibility," but "they are statements of religious convictions, drawn from the Scriptures, and are not to be used to hamper freedom of thought or investigation in other realms of life."

As you shall see in the next chapter, the 1925 Memphis Confession was slightly revised and adopted by the Southern Baptist Convention of Kansas City in 1963. Herschel H. Hobbs of Oklahoma was chairman of the committee that presented the 1963 Kansas City Confession. He underscored the fact that the introductory statements were as much a part of the overall statement as the articles of faith. He added, "If this be denied or ignored, then the statement becomes a creed"[16]—and Baptists are a non-creedal people.

While Baptists traditionally have opposed binding creeds, they have nonetheless adopted periodic "confessions" or "declarations" of their faith. Therefore, the Southern Baptist Convention meeting in 1925 had ample denominational precedent for their actions. The 1925 committee said,

The present occasion for a reaffirmation of Christian fundamentals is the prevalence of naturalism in the modern teaching and preaching of religion. We repudiate every theory of religion which denies the supernatural elements in our faith.

E. Y. Mullins' hand was certainly present in those statements. In his previous statements he had carefully described the issue as supernaturalism versus naturalism. He avoided making the issue more specific, as between scientific evolution and the Bible.

By reading the committee's report, you could almost bet that one member of the committee, C. P. Stealey, was not satisfied. Article 3 of the Confession was not specific enough for him. It read: "Man was created by the special act of God, as recorded in Genesis." On the Convention floor Stealey proposed the following amendment:

We believe man came into the world, by direct creation of God, and not by evolution. This creative act was separate and distinct from any other work of God and was not conditioned upon antecedent changes in previously created forms of life.[17]

The amendment failed to pass, and Article 3 of the Confession stood as presented.

Strife continued. The J. Frank Norris–C. P. Stealey wing of the Convention wanted a more explicit denial of the evolution theory than the Southern Baptist Convention had been willing to give. When the Convention met in Houston in 1926, George W. McDaniel, pastor of First Baptist Church in Richmond, Virginia, was president. He concluded a message to the Convention with the following words:

This Convention accepts Genesis as teaching that man was the special creation of God, and rejects every theory, evolution or other, which teaches that man originated in, or came by way of, a lower animal ancestry.[18]

M. E. Dodd, of First Baptist Church in Shreveport, Louisiana, moved that McDaniel's statement on the subject of evolution and the origin of humans be adopted as the sentiment of the Convention. It was the most unambiguous statement the convention had adopted on the issue, but the avid Fundamentalists were not finished. Even though Dodd's motion included the suggestion that no more attention be given to the evolution issue, more was to come.

On the fourth day of the Convention, a messenger from Arkansas, S. E. Tull, secured the adoption of a resolution that called for all employees of Southern Baptist agencies and institutions to subscribe to the McDaniel statement. Little wonder that the headlines in J. Frank Norris' paper shouted:

"SOUTHERN BAPTIST CONVENTION HEROICALLY AND TRIUMPHANTLY DELIVERS KNOCKOUT BLOW AGAINST EVOLUTION AND EVOLUTIONISTS."

Traces of the evolution controversy appeared for a couple of years, but after the Houston convention, most of the "umph" of it all was gone. By the end of the decade, Southern Baptists were not arguing over evolution. How or why did peace come? Peace came because the Norris-Stealey faction got what it wanted. The Convention spoke to the problem of evolution, it spoke decisively, and it spoke what this group wanted to hear. In a very real sense, the McDaniel statement amended Article 3 of the Memphis Confession of 1925.

The financial condition of the Southern Baptist Convention may have hastened harmony within the ranks. Just prior to the eruption of the evolution controversy, Southern Baptists adopted the Seventy-Five Million Campaign—an effort to raise $75,000,000, between 1919 and 1924. The campaign fell way short. Surely the controversy was not the only, not even the major, reason for the flop; but it was, doubtless, a contributing factor.

Finally, peace came because of the growing disrepute of Fundamentalists such as Norris. About two months after the 1926 Convention, Norris killed Chipps in his church office. Many Southern Baptists had already come to resent J. Frank Norris' hobby: "tending to the Convention." The Chipps incident did not elevate Norris in the eyes of the average Southern Baptist.

Debate, theological and otherwise, continues in Baptist circles. A good bet is that it always shall. How are we to evaluate this heritage? What can we learn? For one thing, we could learn to use cautiously such phrases as "the historic Baptist position." One is on safer ground with "the majority Baptist position." When one asks, "What do Baptists believe about such and such?" one must counter with "which Baptists and in which period?"

The complexity and variety of Baptist thought is one reason, I suppose, why Baptist scholars have never written a book entitled *Baptist Theology.* If Baptists were a people who had tied their souls to a permanent creed, Baptist thought would be easier to delineate. At least three basic ideas have contributed to the diversity in Baptist life. One is the emphasis on the freedom of the individual. A second is the idea of congregational church government. Third, Baptists have made much of "the leadership of the Spirit of God." Diversity and freedom are inherent in that idea.

In Baptist life, debate is possible. No single voice—however so informed, illiterate, or influential—can stifle dissent in a democratic body. That there are problems in such a free-wheeling approach is obvious, but it is a logical outgrowth of the concept of individual worth and freedom.

We need to be reminded that orthopraxy (right practice) is every bit as important as orthodoxy (right teaching). A person who believes right and shouts down another is wrong, no matter what he or she believes. Last of all, we would do well to remind ourselves that "majority rule" does not necessarily produce the will of God.

Notes

[1]For an excellent background discussion of the Fundamentalist-Modernist Controversy see especially pages 3-46 of Willard B. Gatewood, Jr., *Controversy in the Twenties: Fundamentalism, Modernism, and Evolution* (Nashville: Vanderbilt University Press, 1969).

[2]A. C. Underwood, *A History of the English Baptists* (London: Carey Kingsgate Press, 1947) 230.

[3]See article on "Fundamentalism" in *Encyclopedia of Southern Baptists*, vol. 1: 515, 516.

[4]See Norman F. Furniss, *The Fundamentalist Controversy, 1918–1931* (New Haven CT: Yale University Press, 1954) 12. These twelve volumes with slight omissions were reprinted in a four-volume edition issued by the Bible Institute of Los Angeles in 1917. The four-volume edition was reprinted in 1970 by Baker Book House, Grand Rapids MI.

[5]For the Canadian Baptist Controversy, see G. Gerald Harrop's article in Davis C. Woolley, ed., *Baptist Advance* (Nashville: Broadman Press, 1964) 170-173.

[6]As quoted in Robert G. Torbet, *A History of the Baptists* (Valley Forge PA: Judson Press, rev. ed., 1963) 430. Torbet introduces one to the controversy among Northern Baptists, as does Furniss.

[7]As quoted in E. Ray Tatum, *Conquest or Failure: Biography of J. Frank Norris* (Dallas TX: Baptist Historical Foundation, 1966) 102.

[8]This account is in Kenneth K. Bailey, *Southern White Protestantism in the Twentieth Century* (New York: Harper & Row) 61.

[9]Tatum, 182.

[10]As quoted in Tatum, 198.

[11]As quoted in Robert A. Baker, *A Baptist Source Book with Particular Reference to Southern Baptists* (Nashville: Broadman Press, 1966) 197.

[12]See Stewart G. Cole, *The History of Fundamentalism* (New York: Harper & Row, 1931, reprinted Hamden CT: Archon Books, 1963) 283.

[13]For quotes in this section see *Southern Baptist Convention Annual*, 1922, 35, 36.

[14]For quotes see *Southern Baptist Convention Annual*, 1923, 19, 20, 46, 62, 63.

[15]As quoted in Bailey, 65, 66.

[16]Herschel H. Hobbs, *The Baptist Faith and Message* (Nashville: Convention Press, 1971) 12.

[17]*Southern Baptist Convention Annual*, 1925, 76.

[18]*Southern Baptist Convention Annual*, 1926, 18.

Chapter 6

The
"What about Genesis?"
Controversy
or
Baptists Argue about
the Bible

Controversy is not something that has happened to Southern Baptists in the past. It is a happening of the present. In fact, no single decade of Southern Baptist history has spawned more serious controversy than the last ten years. During this period we have argued about many things, but mostly we have argued about biblical interpretation, especially the book of Genesis.

In the early 1960s Southern Baptists were preoccupied with the Elliott Controversy. In the very last months of 1969 and the early 1970s it was the Broadman Commentary Controversy. Both of these controversies focused on biblical and theological interpretation. Specifically, divergent interpretations of the book of Genesis constitute the major area of disagreement. While the Elliott and Broadman Commentary controversies rocked Southern Baptists within the same ten-year period, and while the book of Genesis constituted the storm center of both battles, they are nonetheless distinct controversies. You should look at them separately; only then can you adequately compare and contrast them.

I

Dr. Ralph H. Elliott, who is now retired from the American Baptist Church, was formerly a Southern Baptist and professor of Old Testament at Midwestern Baptist Theological Seminary in Kansas City. He wrote a book that ignited a controversy among Southern Baptists. The controversy eventually led to the dismissal of Elliott from his teaching post.

Entitled *The Message of Genesis*, Elliott's book was, as he stated in his preface,

an effort to combine head and heart by using the sound achievements
of modern scholarship to ferret out and to underscore the foundational
theological and religious principles of the stories of Genesis.

He wanted to skirt the twin dangers of a heartless scholarship and a head-
less religion.

Broadman Press, the book publishing arm of Southern Baptists'
Sunday School board, released 4,000 copies of the book in July, 1961—
in the heat of the year. Was the temperature an omen of things to come?
Surely not, but one great big fire of a controversy came from the publication of the book. Criticism toward Elliott's biblical interpretation came
quickly. Some Baptist editors, pastors, and state denominational workers
exposed what they considered to be the liberal theology of Elliott.

In an interview six years after the controversy, Elliott was asked
which part of the book received the most criticism. He answered, "My
comments about the first eleven chapters of Genesis, in which I suggested we are dealing with theological fact, not day-by-day physical history."
When asked what were some of the key questions that he raised in the
book, the ex-professor said,

> the seven days of creation. The most bitter critics felt God created the
> earth in seven literal twenty-four-hour days. I just cannot buy this. And
> there was a question of whether Adam was just one man, or if he repre-
> sents mankind. I raised the possibility the answer was mankind.[1]

Whereas Professor Elliott considered Genesis 1–11 (the story of creation, of Adam, the garden, the flood, the tower, and so on) symbolic, his
critics insisted upon the literal and historical nature of these accounts.
Whereas Elliott felt that the essential message of the Genesis (note the
title of his book) material was not diminished but enriched by a symbolic
interpretation, his opponents believed that the trustworthiness of the Bible
depended on the historical accuracy of the material. To be sure, these
were not the only issues of dispute, but they were among the most commonly mentioned areas of disagreement.

Pointing out what he considered to be the gravity of the situation, one
critic, writing in the 9 September 1961 issue of the Kansas *Baptist
Digest*, said:

Southern Baptists are at the crossroads in the publication of this book. In this book we are not facing a matter of ecclesiology or polity. This concerns the very heart of the gospel. It is an undercutting of the doctrine of revelation.

Many Southern Baptists agreed.

One of the most publicized criticisms of Elliott's book was published in the 10 January 1962, issue of *The Baptist Standard*, the Texas Baptist paper. K. Owen White, then pastor of First Baptist Church in Houston, wrote the article that he entitled, ". . . Death in the Pot." After quoting several passages from Elliott's work, White described it as "liberalism, pure and simple." He added,

The book in question is "poison." This sort of rationalistic criticism can lead only to further confusion, unbelief, deterioration, and ultimately disintegration as a great New Testament denomination.

White suggested that people of Elliott's viewpoint should be invited to find a place of service outside Southern Baptist life. He also asked trustees of the seminaries to exercise caution in approving faculty members and urged the Sunday School Board to be more alert to liberalism in Baptist publications.

Elliott was not without support. Appearing in the same issue of *The Baptist Standard* alongside White's negative evaluation was a positive critique by Robert H. Craft, a Kansas pastor. In his highly complimentary view of Elliott's work Craft said, "The author leads the reader through an exhilarating and fruitful study of the delicate problems conservative scholars have too long neglected in the study of Genesis." One month later in the 15 February issue of the *Arkansas Baptist Newsmagazine*, Charles Trentham, pastor of First Baptist Church in Knoxville, Tennessee, praised Elliott's work for preserving

the true spiritual values of the Genesis narrative so that no honest student need feel that he is intellectually dishonest when he contends that there still is an honest harmony between science and religion.

In late 1961 the Board of Trustees at Midwestern Seminary passed a resolution affirming confidence in Elliott "as a consecrated Christian, a promising scholar and teacher, a loyal servant of Southern Baptists, and a dedicated and warmly evangelistic preacher of the gospel."

On the heels of the action by the Midwestern Board of Trustees, the fifty-four-member Sunday School Board met in Nashville, 29-31 January 1962, for its semiannual meeting. A statement of position was adopted concerning the publication by Broadman Press of Elliott's book. The statement emphasized that *The Message of Genesis* was published for use as resource material for seminary students (one of the very things that critics of the book abhorred) and for in-depth Bible study.

Furthermore, the Sunday School Board stated that Broadman Press recognized that the point of view expressed in the book would not be acceptable to all Southern Baptists, but they contended that unanimity of acceptance was not a criteria for publication of a manuscript. The Sunday School Board urged Broadman Press, therefore, to continue to publish books that would present more than one point of view. Finally, the Sunday School Board declared that

> Broadman Press ministers to the denomination in keeping with the historic Baptist principle of the freedom of the individual to interpret the Bible for himself, to hold a particular theory of inspiration of the Bible which seems most reasonable to him, and to develop his beliefs in accordance with his theory.[2]

Neither the praise that the pro-Elliott fans could muster nor the rationale given by the Sunday School Board could silence the issue. While it is impossible to know precisely how many Southern Baptists were "for" or "against" Elliott's viewpoints, the majority was undoubtably "against." Salvador T. Martinez made a careful study of the reactions of twenty-eight Southern Baptist newspapers and editors. Of the twenty-eight he said sixteen were unfavorable toward Elliott, five were favorable, four were uncommitted but would likely oppose Elliott, and three were uncommitted but would likely support Elliott.[3]

When Southern Baptists met for their annual convention in San Francisco in June, 1962, everybody knew that the big issue was "the Elliott thing." In March before the June convention an informal group of Baptist pastors, denominational workers, and laymen—critics of Elliott's book—met in Oklahoma City. They had met to discuss what they considered to be "the current theological crisis within the denomination." According to a 16 March 1962, Baptist Press news release, the "apparent immediate objective" of the group was to secure the election of theologically conservative men to the Board of Trustees of Midwestern Seminary.

This meeting was condemned by some Baptist editors, and approved by others. Erwin L. McDonald of the *Arkansas Baptist Newsmagazine* objected by saying, "Surely we do not need anything that might remotely resemble a spiritual version of the Ku Klux Klan." James F. Cole of the Louisiana paper, while not referring specifically to the Oklahoma meeting, warned his readers of the danger of "the society of authoritative dogmatism" as well as of "liberalism." E. S. James of *The Baptist Standard* defended the meeting at Oklahoma City and decried the charge of Ku Kluxism.[4]

The Oklahoma City meeting represented the seriousness with which Southern Baptists were viewing the Elliott controversy. Prior to the 1962 San Francisco Convention, Baptist papers were filled with articles examining every facet of the controversy. No one knew exactly what would happen at San Francisco, but the messengers arrived in the Bay area expecting a showdown.

Before the four-day convention concluded, five resolutions were presented that related to Ralph Elliott, the seminaries' boards of trustees, and the Sunday School Board. The first of these was a recommendation presented by the Executive Committee of the Convention. It called for the appointment of a special committee to present a confessional statement, similar to the 1925 Memphis Confession, to the 1963 Southern Baptist Convention in Kansas City. Obviously some leaders hoped that the adoption of such a recommendation would de-fuse the Elliott bomb in San Francisco. The recommendation passed, and the committee was appointed; but the fire was not out.[5]

The second and third motions pertaining to the fuss were presented by K. Owen White of Houston. One of these, adopted unanimously, said: "That the messengers to this Convention, by standing vote, reaffirm their faith in the *entire* Bible as the authoritative, authentic, infallible Word of God." In the other White resolution, passed by a large majority, the messengers to the Convention declared:

> That we express our abiding and unchanging objection to the dissemination of theological views in any of our seminaries which would undermine such faith in the historical accuracy and doctrinal integrity of the Bible, and that

we courteously request the Trustees and administrative officers of our institutions and other agencies to take such steps as shall be necessary to remedy at once those situations where such views now threaten our historic position.[6]

A fourth motion presented by Ralph F. Powell of Missouri called for the Sunday School Board to stop publishing and "recall from all sales" *The Message of Genesis*. This motion was later withdrawn by Mr. Powell. Shortly after Powell withdrew his motion, a messenger from Oregon presented a similar proposal instructing "the Sunday School Board to cease publishing and to recall from all distribution channels, the book, *The Message of Genesis*." The motion was defeated, so the Convention refused to ban Elliott's book. But the Sunday School Board, due to an administrative decision, never republished the book.

Following the San Francisco Convention, the complexion and attitude of Midwestern Seminary's board of trustees changed. Some obviously interpreted the action of the Southern Baptist Convention as a mandate to dismiss Elliott. A special committee of the board consulted with Elliott and the seminary administration. Agreement was reached concerning principles relating to biblical teaching, including the historical-critical method. The difference of opinion that led to Elliott's dismissal was over the republication of *The Message of Genesis*. The committee wanted Elliott to promise not to republish the book. He refused. He was then dismissed, not because of heresy, but because of insubordination.[7] As Davis C. Woolley said, "Elliott left Midwestern a victim of the controversy yet without the brand of a heretic."[8]

What were the results of the controversy? A couple are obvious. For one thing, a professor lost his job. Critics of Elliott saw it as a victory for theological conservatism; supporters of Elliott saw it as a tragic injustice. Secondly, Southern Baptists adopted a Confession of Faith in Kansas City in 1963. Yet, the adoption of the Confession was anti-climatic because Elliott was gone by the time of the 1963 Convention. A third and less obvious result of the discussion was an intensification and popularization of the suspicion of theological education and publications. A fourth result was that a young seminary, established only in 1958, encountered a serious injury in its infancy.

II

Elliott left, but the problem remained. Only eight years after the stormy San Francisco convention, Southern Baptists convened and had an even stormier session over Genesis. This time it was in Denver, Colorado, in June, 1970. The issue at stake was the recently published Volume 1 of *The Broadman Bible Commentary*. The specific concern was the interpretation of the book of Genesis.

The Broadman Bible Commentary, a projected twelve-volume set of commentaries on the entire Bible, was conceived in 1957, approved by the elected Sunday School Board in 1961, and "designed for those who feel a need for a more thoughtful type of work, probing in depth into the truths of God's word."[9] Volume 1 of the commentary contained (1) general articles on the Bible; and (2) an exposition of Genesis by G. Henton Davies, an English Baptist, (the Elliott Controversy may have helped the editors decide on a non-Southern Baptist writer for Genesis) and an exposition of Exodus by Roy L. Honeycutt, Professor of Old Testament at Midwestern Seminary.

Published in October, 1969, the commentary was expected to draw some criticism. In the 11 September 1969 issue of *The California Southern Baptist*, editor J. Terry Young issued a word of commendation and a word of caution even before Volume 1 was released. He commended the Sunday School Board and Broadman Press for publishing "this significant set." Then he added, "We don't know who will get to read the first copy off the press, but we confidently expect that he will find something in it with which he disagrees," but he argued that some diversity of interpretation is expected in the denomination because "that's the nature of us Baptists." He warned his readers that they would doubtless hear an assortment of criticisms of the commentaries, but he admonished individual Southern Baptists to form opinions on the basis of personal study and not the reaction of someone else.

Few, if any, anticipated as much dissatisfaction with the commentary as was finally expressed at the Denver Convention. State Baptist papers began editorializing and carrying articles and reviews of the commentary. Responses to the commentary varied; some applauded, others were cautious, and still others were decidedly negative.

One of the earliest published criticisms of Volume 1 of the Broadman Commentary came from W. Ross Edwards, editor of *Word and Way*, the

Missouri Baptist paper. In the 8 January 1970 issue of his paper, Edwards wrote an editorial entitled "Witnessing to the Truth," which he described as "Part 1 of a review of the Broadman Bible commentary." He declared that the two recently-released volumes of the Broadman Commentary were "well written and, in the main, conservative," but went on to say "that the writings of Dr. G. Henton Davies in the volume on Genesis are too liberal for most Southern Baptists."

Edwards' major criticism of Davies was in the English scholar's interpretation of Genesis 22:1-19, the story of Abraham's proposed sacrifice of Isaac. In his discussion of the passage, Davies acknowledged that some interpreters accepted literally the command to Abraham to sacrifice Isaac. Davies queried, "Did God make, would God in fact have made, such a demand upon Abraham or anybody else, except himself?" Davies then answered the question with the following paragraph

> Our answer however is no. Indeed what Christian or humane conscience could regard such a command as coming from God? How then did this conviction arise in the mind of Abraham, since we believe that God did not put it there? The question can only be answered in part. Abraham's conviction that his son must be sacrificed is the climax of the psychology of his life.[10]

This became the most widely disputed interpretation in the commentary, and Edwards was one of the first to attack it. Edwards closed his editorial by saying,

> the writings of Dr. Davies are not suitable for 'a mighty army marching forth to victory.' He sounds more like a drummer boy beating a retreat. . . . We believe that Southern Baptists cannot grow spiritually on a diet like Dr. Davies offers. I'm not prepared to "eat it." How about you?

A week after Edwards' editorial, the editor of *The Baptist Messenger* of Oklahoma wrote an editorial entitled "Warning to Our People." He, too, zeroed-in on Davies' handling of the Abraham-Isaac event. He said: "The book is a deep disappointment. Don't waste your money buying it. Don't waste your time reading it."

In the 5 March 1970 edition of the state Baptist paper of Tennessee, J. Wash Watts, former Professor of Hebrew and Old Testament at New Orleans Baptist Theological Seminary, wrote on "Conflicts Between the

Treatment of Genesis in the Broadman Bible Commentary and the Bible Itself." Watts declared that Davies' interpretation of Genesis 22 "casts dark doubt on the word of the Bible." Rhetorically he asked, "Can Southern Baptists remain loyal to their confession of faith in the inspiration of the Bible and promote a treatment that abuses it as this one does?"

Just as Ralph Elliott had some support from Southern Baptists, so did the Broadman Commentary. "In Defense of the Broadman Bible Commentary" was the title of an editorial by C. R. Daley, Jr. in the Kentucky Baptist paper. "With Dr. Davies and his critics it is the same old story of literalism versus nonliteralism," Daley said. He pointed out that one could differ with Davies' interpretation of the Bible without accusing the scholar of denying the inspiration of the Bible. Daley also said that "the only way to satisfy every critic would be to let each critic write his own commentary."[11]

The Southern Baptist Convention met in Denver 1-4 June. On 30 May, just prior to the convention, a group of Southern Baptists met in what was called the "Affirming the Bible Conference." The announcement of such a conference was issued by Ross Edwards on 12 March. He declared that a vocal minority of liberals had "challenged Bible-believing Baptists" ever since the 1962 Southern Baptist Convention in San Francisco. The conference on "Affirming the Bible" was called, according to Edwards, because "we want Southern Baptist liberals to know that there is a limit to our patience."[12] Some attributed what they called the noisy and militant Southern Baptist Convention of Denver to a negative influence issuing from this conference.

The motion that produced the most stir at the 1970 Southern Baptist Convention was presented by Gwin T. Turner of California. He moved

> that because the new *The Broadman Commentary* is out of keeping with the beliefs of the vast majority of Southern Baptist pastors and people this Convention requests the Sunday School Board to withdraw Volume 1 from further distribution and that it be rewritten with due consideration of the conservative viewpoint.[13]

In his criticism of the commentary, Turner claimed that it directly contradicted the Bible. He referred specifically to the Abraham-Isaac sacrifice episode. James L. Sullivan, executive-secretary of the Sunday School Board, defended the publication of the book by saying (1) that no book produced by Broadman Press is considered to be the official position of the Southern Baptist Convention and (2) that the board produced books for various segments of Southern Baptists.

Clifton J. Allen, general editor of the commentary, pled with the messengers to the Denver Convention, "Let us pass on to the next generation a heritage of the open mind and open Bible, to understand and interpret it under the leadership of the Holy Spirit." The plea was in vain; the motion to withdraw and rewrite the commentary passed 5,394 to 2,170.

Two months following the Southern Baptist Convention the elected members of the Sunday School Board met at Glorieta, New Mexico, August 11-13. In keeping with the request of the Southern Baptist Convention, the board voted by a two-to-one margin to withdraw Volume 1 of the Broadman Commentary from distribution and sale. The Board also named a special committee to make suggestions for re-writing the commentary from a conservative viewpoint.

When the Sunday School Board met in Nashville in January 1971, the special committee recommended that the authors of the Genesis and Exodus sections of the commentary be asked to rewrite their material. An amendment to the committee's report was adopted which asked the authors to accept "the task of rewriting Volume 1 of the commentary with due consideration of the conservative viewpoint." The phrase "with due consideration of the conservative viewpoint" was a part of the motion adopted by the Denver convention in June, 1970.[14]

It looked like the commentary would be rewritten by the same authors. But not so, at least not for the Genesis commentary. Some Southern Baptists felt the Sunday School Board had not done what the Denver Convention asked. So at the St. Louis Convention in June, 1971, the following motion passed by a majority of 2,672 to 2,290:

> That the Sunday School Board be advised that the vote of the 1970 Convention regarding the rewriting of Volume 1 of the Broadman Commentary has not been followed and that the Sunday School Board obtain another writer and proceed with the commentary according to the vote of the 1970 convention in Denver.

Several points need to be noted here. (1) The Sunday School Board thought by getting Davies and Honeycutt to revise the commentary, the convention action of 1970 was being followed. (2) It was obvious that the major area of concern was not the Exodus section of the volume but the Genesis portion. The motion adopted in St. Louis called for the Sunday School Board to "obtain another writer." This was an obvious reference to Davies, although even this fact was not spelled out in the 1971 motion. (3) While the messengers to the convention vetoed Davies as the author of the Genesis section of the commentary, the vote was close. It won by a 382-vote margin. In contrast, however, the motion to rewrite the commentary won by a 3,224-vote margin. A greater percentage of Southern Baptists felt free to vote for the rewriting than felt free to dictate to the Sunday School Board how or who should do the rewriting. Yet, the majority still wanted a new writer.

The elected trustees of the Sunday School Board met in July at Ridgecrest, North Carolina, and the following motion was approved by a vote of 34–21:

> In response to the action of the Southern Baptist Convention in St. Louis regarding Volume 1 of the Broadman Bible Commentary, we request and authorize the administration to seek to secure a new author for the commentary on the text of Genesis, also to report to the January meeting of the board the progress achieved and any developments or complications calling for further direction or authorization by the board.[15]

At the original writing of this book, that is where the Broadman Commentary Controversy stood. Since then, the administration of the Sunday School Board was authorized to select a new writer for the Genesis volume: Clyde Francisco.

III

An in-depth analysis of the Elliott and Broadman controversies would make an interesting comparative study. Some bright-eyed graduate student ought to jump on it. For one thing, both controversies were stimulated by diverse interpretations of Genesis. In both controversies, "liberals" and "conservatives" accepted and affirmed the Bible as God's Word. However, "conservatives" claimed that to deny the historicity of biblical events (or to refuse to take the Bible literally) is the same as denying the

Bible as the reliable Word of God. "Liberals," on the other hand, said the important thing about the Bible is its message, not its literary nature.

One of the obvious contrasts in these two controversies is that the 1962 Southern Baptist Convention refused to ban Elliott's book, while the 1970 Convention voted overwhelmingly to request the Sunday School Board to withdraw the Broadman Commentary. Why? Perhaps can only guess and offer the guesses to others. One, some Southern Baptist leaders who were strongly opposed to Elliott were just as strongly opposed to banning Elliott's book. E. S. James, for example, editor of the Texas Baptist paper and staunch Elliott critic, described the 1962 motion to withdraw *The Message of Genesis* as "unnecessary," "extreme," and "coercive." He said, "Let's have our agencies free to make decisions, and let's criticize them if they make wrong ones."[16] That attitude prevailed in 1962, but not in 1970.

Secondly, the 1962 Convention was afflicted with only one explosive issue: the Elliott Controversy. The 1970 Convention had two other trouble spots in addition to the Broadman argument. One of these was the furor that had erupted over the Atlanta Morality Seminar, sponsored by the Christian Life Commission of the Southern Baptist Convention. The second was a general concern on the part of some regarding the alleged "liberal" tendencies of the Sunday School and Training Union literature. In a sense, there were just too many fires for the influential leadership of the Convention to put out in 1970. The fact that there were several fires and not just one aggravated the atmosphere.

Three, in the Elliott Controversy, the issue could be personalized and focused on Ralph Elliott, a man employed by a Southern Baptist institution. In the Broadman Controversy, however, the issue could not be personalized: Henton Davies was an English Baptist. The result? In the first controversy the spotlight was on a man; in the second, a book. Yet, both controversies were at bottom biblical and theological.

Notes

[1]See Roy Jennings, "Ralph Elliott: Six Years After *The Message of Genesis*," *Baptist Men's Journal* (April-May-June 1968): 6.

[2]For this statement see *The Baptist Standard*, 7 February 1962; *Baptist and Reflector*, 8 February 1962; *The Religious Herald*, 15 February 1962; and other state Baptist papers.

[3]Salvador T. Martinez, "Southern Baptist Views of the Scriptures in Light of the Elliott Controversy" (Th.M. thesis, Southern Baptist Theological Seminary, 1966), 179, 180. Microfilm print, Dargan-Carver Library, Nashville.

[4]For editorial positions on the Oklahoma Meeting see *The Baptist Standard*, 30 May 1962; *The Baptist Message*, 15 March 1962; and *Arkansas Baptist Newsmagazine*, 22 March 1962.

[5]For a good discussion of the background and results of this recommendation, see Herschel H. Hobbs, *The Baptist Faith and Message* (Nashville: Convention Press, 1971) 13-17.

[6]*Southern Baptist Convention Annual*, 1962, 65, 68.

[7]See Baptist Press News Releases for 28 October 1962, and 29 October 1962, in Dargan-Carver Library, Baptist Sunday School Board, Nashville TN.

[8]Davis C. Woolley, "Major Convention Crises over a Century and a Quarter," *Review and Expositor* (Spring 1970): 179.

[9]James L. Sullivan, "Why the Broadman Commentary Was Published," *Western Recorder*, 11 April 1970, 11.

[10]G. Henton Davies, "Genesis," *The Broadman Bible Commentary*, vol. 1 (Nashville: Broadman Press, 1969) 198.

[11]See *Western Recorder*, 11 April 1970, 4.

[12]*The Word and Way*, 12 March 1970, 2.

[13]*Southern Baptist Convention Annual*, 1970, 63.

[14]For a full report of this meeting of the Sunday School Board see *Baptist and Reflector*, 4 February 1971, 8.

[15]See Baptist Press News Release, 23 July 1971.

[16]See Martinez, 28, 29.

Chapter 7

The
Fundamentalist-Moderate
Controversy
or
Baptists Argue about
Almost Everything

"We will have a great time here, if for no other reason than to elect Adrian Rogers our president."

Those apparently casual, throw-away words by W. A. Criswell during the introductory comments to his sermon at the SBC Pastor's Conference in Houston, Texas, on 11 June 1979, brought the SBC house down with cheers and applause. More pessimistic observers would simply say those words brought the SBC house down! Not really, however.

Dissected fifteen years later with the benefit of hindsight, the words of the famous pastor of First Baptist Church, Dallas, Texas, contained significance unimaginable that night in Houston. In terms of future SBC leadership, those words introduced Adrian Rogers, the person most responsible for the transformation of the Southern Baptist identity over the next decade. Moreover, those words prophetically, if unknowingly, symbolized the passing of the mantle of fundamentalist leadership in Southern Baptist life from Criswell to Rogers.

In terms of future SBC politics, Criswell's words meant that gentlemen's agreements were no longer operative. Heretofore, former SBC presidents, of which Criswell was one, refrained from public endorsements of possible candidates for national SBC offices. Criswell broke that code of conduct. But many rules of SBC civility would be raucously shattered before the decade of the eighties closed for, on that night in Houston, Southern Baptists were on the verge of the "mother" and "father" of all Baptist controversies.

In a historical sense, Criswell's words marked the first installment in the transformation of the SBC from a conservative to a fundamentalist denomination. In terms of the denominational controversy that ensued, Criswell's words are as good as any to signal publicly the firing of the first official salvo in the wrenching and decade-long struggle for the control of the largest Protestant denomination in America.

Criswell proved to be a prophet when he said, "We will have a great time here." Criswell's crowd did indeed have a great time in Houston in 1979. On the first day of the SBC meeting that year, messengers to the convention elected Adrian Rogers as president, over five other candidates, on the first ballot with 51.36% of the vote. A first ballot presidential election in the SBC was rare, if not unheard of. Criswell's crowd also had "a great time" for the rest of the decade, successfully electing fundamentalist presidential candidates for the next eleven years over moderate rivals. Did these presidential elections change anything in SBC life? Almost everything! They changed almost everything because Southern Baptists during this decade argued about almost everything.

I

Before exploring chronological details of the most serious controversy in the history of the SBC, you need an overview so you can get your bearings.[1] Two factions, Fundamentalists and Moderates, polarized the SBC from 1979–1990. While the war at the national SBC level between the rival parties ended in 1990, fallout persists to the writing of these lines in the spring of 1995. A good bet is that debris will continue to fall at national, state, and local church levels for several years to come.

With numerous antecedents, the conflict began in earnest on 12-14 June 1979, at the annual meeting of the SBC in Houston, Texas. Three fundamentalist leaders emerged prominently at that meeting and skillfully guided the Fundamentalists to triumph over Moderates for twelve years. Those three were Paige Patterson, then president of Criswell Center for Biblical Studies in Dallas, Texas; Paul Pressler, a layman from Houston, Texas; and Adrian Rogers, pastor of Bellevue Baptist Church in Memphis, Tennessee. Each man served a crucial role in the fundamentalist victory. Patterson, a professor, was the theological architect; Pressler, a judge, was the political strategist; and Rogers, an effective and popular preacher without whom the Fundamentalists probably never would have won, stirred to action mass SBC audiences.

Beginning in the spring of 1979, Pressler and Patterson designed and announced a ten-year plan whereby Fundamentalists could gain political control of the Southern Baptist Convention. Garnering a following by proclaiming that "liberalism" had invaded the entire denominational system—seminaries, colleges, universities, publication agencies, denominational press, and almost all of the national boards and agencies—they discovered that they could use the appointive powers of the SBC presidency and thereby dominate the denomination.

Indeed, the Fundamentalist-Moderate Controversy has been more serious for Southern Baptists than any of the three previous controversies of the twentieth century because the Fundamentalists of the 1980s interpreted the problem to be systemic, not singular or isolated. In contrast, the Norrisite controversy focused on a single issue—evolution; the Genesis Controversy focused on a single person—Ralph Elliott; and the Broadman Controversy focused on a single book—volume one of a commentary series.

Following the 1979 election of Adrian Rogers as SBC president, all of the seven presidents through the election in 1990 were Fundamentalists who used their presidential powers to achieve the fundamentalist agenda by stacking the boards of all trustee agencies, something never done in SBC history. By 1990, hardliners dominated virtually every SBC agency's board of trustees, the control mechanisms of the denomination.

They did not do it, however, without a mighty struggle, as the percentages for the presidential election will verify.[2] A resistance movement to the fundamentalizing of the SBC began on 25 September 1980 in Gatlinburg, Tennessee. Encouraged by Duke K. McCall—SBC patriarch and longtime president of the Southern Baptist Theological Seminary in Louisville, Kentucky—Cecil Sherman—the lanky, slow-talking, fast-thinking pastor of the First Baptist Church, Asheville, North Carolina—called the Gatlinburg meeting, galvanized the resistance movement, and became the single most important moderate leader throughout the conflict. Ken Chafin, James Slatton, Daniel Vestal, and many others were important to the moderate cause, but Sherman's courageous voice called the movement into being and stayed at the moderate helm for most of the decade. After the controversy ended and the Moderates organized the Cooperative Baptist Fellowship, Moderates called on Cecil Sherman to spearhead the new Baptist organization.

While the political key to the fundamentalist victory throughout the decade was the election of the SBC president and subsequent trustee appointments, the fundamentalist rallying cry was "the inerrancy of the Bible." The popular name of the controversy became "The Inerrancy

Controversy." While the Bible was a central issue, the strife focused on far, far more than either the nature or interpretation of the Bible, so the conflict should be known as the "Fundamentalist-Moderate Controversy."

Even the word "controversy" may be too tame and tepid a word for what happened. Everybody asked during the controversy, and they continue to ask, "What was the issue? Why the explosion?" Fundamentalists want you to believe that it was simply a matter that they believed the Bible and Moderates did not. That was and is humbug, though there is certainly a difference between the two groups regarding the Bible.

Moderates, on the other hand, interpreted the conflict in the early years almost exclusively as a political grab for power, an exercise in ecclesiastical piracy by people who had never paid their share of the denominational bills, nurtured denominational institutions, or participated in denominational programs. That was shortsighted, though history confirms that it obviously contained an enormous truth. As events unfolded, Fundamentalists desired exceedingly more than the "parity" they claimed they wanted in the early years. They wanted a tight-fisted control of the denomination, without Moderates.

Historians and observers of the battle have numerous interpretations of what it was all about. Now that some dust has settled we still have to squint, but maybe we see a bit more clearly. What happened was a clash of Baptist cultures, and the "Baptist" part of the culture clash is crucial. The SBC fight of the 1980s was not merely a reflection of the larger culture war going on in America at that time. Specific "Baptist" ingredients made the SBC struggle distinct. For example, some persons identified with the moderate cause were theologically comfortable with the Fundamentalists. Why then identify with Moderates? The answer: because of the "Baptist" ingredients in the struggle. These ingredients as detailed below included what historians call the "voluntary principle" in religion and the cardinal Baptist distinctives evolving from that principle: the priesthood of all believers, anti-creedalism, congregational autonomy, religious liberty, and separation of church and state.

Make no mistake, however. While it was Baptist, it was a Baptist "culture-clash," a head-on collision between rival ideologies and conflicting visions. Conflicting visions of what? As I said earlier, of almost everything. Cecil Sherman and Paige Patterson, for example, had differences that, as Diane Winston accurately said, "began with theology but spilled into worldviews that diverged on everything from political issues to denominational structures."[3]

Winston, a non-Baptist, has written one of the best, brief, non-technical, journalistic accounts of the controversy. While a journalistic and not historically precise account, and while the contrast would have been better had she used Rogers rather than Patterson, Winston does a good job of introducing one to the conflicting visions of the Fundamentalists and the Moderates. The reader must also understand that Patterson did not speak for all Fundamentalists nor Sherman for all Moderates, but Winston's contrast of Patterson and Sherman lets one "feel" the difference in the two groups.

> For Patterson, the Baptist is first and last a soul winner bound to the irrefutable word of God. God's word supersedes all else—in fact, it shapes all of life. God's word dictates political stands—opposing abortion and the ERA, fighting godless communism and strengthening a Christian America; it clarifies ecclesiastical choices—building larger churches and bringing in more lost souls; it advances theological positions—banning women ministers and opting for evangelism, rather than dialogue, with other religions. Patterson's is a rigorous system demanding adherence to an all-or-nothing faith. It is also an ideology that coincided with the then-reigning sensibility in American life. Like Reaganism it vaunted the triumph of the chosen, as evidenced in outward signs of election: bigger, better, richer.
>
> Cecil Sherman's understanding of Baptist life has fewer sharper edges. The Baptist is bound to the Bible, but each human being is free to interpret Scripture. Denominational life is not undergirded by creed but by freely given cooperation in missions and educational work. Religious life is a rich weave of faith-driven individuals seeking God in their own way. Moderates may not like abortion, but they recognize it may be necessary in some cases. They believe the Baptist way is right, but they will listen to a Jew or Muslim. They can appreciate big and beautiful sanctuaries, but they say teaching believers to live Christian lives is as important as saving souls.[4]

One attitude, generic in character, hung as a colossal canopy over all the contention. That attitude was "control versus freedom," no new conflict in Baptist history. Fundamentalists argued for stricter controls in light of what they believed was too much freedom that had issued in false teachings. Moderates, on the other hand, lobbied for freedom in the face of what they thought was a non-Baptistic and paralyzing control. This central issue may also be described as "conformity versus liberty" or "uniformity versus diversity." Fundamentalists were interested in theological conformity and denominational uniformity. Moderates were interested in liberty of conscience and denominational diversity.

The "control versus freedom" war played itself out in numerous smaller battles. Biblically, the two groups disputed the nature and interpretation of the Bible. Fundamentalists argued that the original documents of the Bible contained no scientific, historical, geographical, or theological errors. This is a theory known as "biblical inerrancy." According to Fundamentalists, if one were not an "inerrantist," one did not believe the Bible, despite the fact that both Paige Patterson and Paul Pressler admitted that we do not have an accurate text of the Bible.[5]

Moderates, on the other hand, contended for the authority of Scripture "for faith and practice" but not as an inerrant scientific and historical book, arguing correctly that we have no original documents of the Bible, only copies. Moderates saw the emphasis on inerrancy as bibliolatry, an unnecessary flirting with idolatry because only God is without error. Moreover, Moderates interpreted the Bible so as to allow for a symbolic interpretation of Adam and Eve, while Fundamentalists viewed this interpretation as denying the truth of the Bible.

Theologically, they wrangled over the role of women and pastoral authority. Fundamentalists insisted on a hierarchical model of male-female relationships and denied a woman's right for ordination to the ministry or the diaconate. Moderates, more egalitarian, advocated equality between women and men and affirmed ordination for women. Fundamentalists embraced pastoral authority in the local church to the point of saying that the pastor was to "rule" the church. Moderates believed any such notion was contrary to the biblical and Baptist heritages and countered with the historic Baptist emphases of the priesthood of all believers and congregational authority.

Educationally, the two parties argued over almost every facet of theological education—content, parameters, personnel, and methodology. Much of the heat of the controversy focused on theological seminaries, especially Southeastern Baptist Theological Seminary in Wake Forest, North Carolina, and Southern Baptist Theological Seminary in Louisville, Kentucky. Before the battle was over, both of these institutions were firmly in the grasp of fundamentalist control and undergoing radical transformation under fundamentalist presidents Paige Patterson at Southeastern and Al Mohler at Southern.

Ethically, the combatants disagreed over the implications of religious liberty and separation of church and state, particularly as those principles related to prayer in public schools, abortion, capital punishment, and related national issues. Most of the energy in the area of ethics was spent in the fundamentalist opposition to and moderate defense of both the SBC's Christian Life Commission and the Baptist Joint Committee on Public Affairs, a national agency based in Washington, D.C., and supported by several Baptist denominations in the United States. Both of these agencies were traditionally strong advocates of religious liberty and strict in their emphasis on the separation of church and state.

Historically and denominationally, the two groups disputed the place of creedalism in Baptist life, the intent and purpose of the SBC (whether missional or doctrinal), and the freedom/control of the denominational press (Baptist Press) and the denominational publishing agency (Baptist Sunday School Board; Broadman Press). Moderates opposed theological creeds, believed the purpose of the SBC was functional, and wanted the Baptist Press and Baptist Sunday School Board free from excessive control. Fundamentalists, on the other hand, while claiming to be noncreedal, centralized and creedalized the SBC to a degree unheard of in Baptist life and pressed for rigid boundaries for the work of the Sunday School Board.

Missiologically, they differed over the theological credentials for missionary appointment and the vocational purposes of missionaries. This particular dimension of the contest focused on the SBC Foreign Mission Board and the Home Mission Board, two of the darling agencies of the denomination.

Politically—in terms of national politics—Fundamentalists identified with the political right-wing, while Moderates tended to be more centrists. For example, Fundamentalists tended to support Reagan-Bush Republicans, and Moderates more generally identified with Carter-Clinton Democrats. To illustrate, after the Fundamentalists gained control of the SBC and the Moderates had organized the Cooperative Baptist Fellowship, Dan Quayle and Oliver North, right-wing Republicans, were celebrated speakers at the SBC while Jimmy Carter spoke at a meeting of the CBF.

The two groups were so divided that they could not even arrive at mutually acceptable names for the rival parties. Both wanted to be called

"Conservatives." Therefore, the term has little value in describing the conflict. In fact, both parties wanted the term so much that at one point the Baptist Press dubbed the adversaries, in the name of fairness, with the cumbersome names of "The Fundamentalist-Conservatives" and "The Moderate-Conservatives." The most accurate terminology is "Fundamentalists" and "Moderates," though neither party likes its appellation.

Fundamentalists were sometimes called "inerrantists," "the takeover group," or "the Pressler-Patterson faction"—after the name of two of their founders. Moderates were sometimes called "liberals," "denominational loyalists," "Baptists Committed," or "traditionalists," because they maintained that they were the traditional Baptists. Since the fundamentalist takeover of the SBC, the Baptist Press always refers to SBC Fundamentalists as "Conservatives."

II

Numerous books and articles have now been written detailing the blow-by-blow accounts.[6] "Blow by blow" is good terminology, for this was a staggering, twelve-round, heavyweight, denominational fight. Looking back, one can discern three distinct phases to it. In the initial phase, the first five rounds (1979–1983), the opponents were—in boxing language—"feeling each other out." The fundamentalist challenger, while never tentative, appeared at times awkward and uncertain of triumph. Likewise, the Moderates, especially denominational agency heads, while exhibiting severe apprehension, believed in the early years that the upstart could be "handled." The second phase lasted from 1984 to 1987. During this period a momentum swing occurred, the decisive momentum change coming in the sixth round in 1984 and intensifying until the SBC meeting in 1988. The third phase, the knock-out rounds, came during 1988–1990. While the bell rang to end the major battle in 1990, "bleacher fights" have occurred almost every year since.

Phase One: 1979–1983

Even though Fundamentalists won every presidential election during the initial five-year period of the controversy, folks on both sides during this initial phase had good reason to be unsure of the long-range outcome. Why? For one thing, history was on the side of the Moderates. Extremists such as J. R. Graves and J. Frank Norris had never been successful. Many people, therefore, within the denomination naively took an "it-can't-happen-here-approach" to the Patterson-Pressler assault in the spring of 1979.

Moreover, as one reviews the early months and years of the controversy, a lull definitely appeared in the fundamentalist attack. The first sign of this lull came in early May 1980 when Adrian Rogers announced he would not seek a second presidential term because of his church responsibilities in Memphis. While that may in fact have been the case, those responsibilities must have slackened in the mid-1980s when Rogers accepted the SBC presidency two more times during the intensifying fundamentalist juggernaut! One wonders if Rogers genuinely believed the takeover was a possibility early on. Maybe Rogers, recognizing the potential for a major denominational wreck, had second thoughts about the entire enterprise.

A second signal of "lull" in fundamentalist momentum came also in May 1980. Fundamentalist patriarch W. A. Criswell, Paige Patterson's pastor and "supervisor" at First Baptist Church in Dallas, announced that Patterson would withdraw from the fundamentalist effort at electing SBC presidents. According to Criswell, the methods adopted by Patterson and others are "those of a different world" that Baptists traditionally disdain. Everybody in the Southern Baptist Convention should have known that something new was in the mix when Criswell could not rein in his younger associate and Paul Pressler.[7]

A third signal of fundamentalist tentativeness came from Rogers in May 1982. In an interview with Jack Harwell, editor of *The Christian Index* at that time, Rogers voiced grave doubt that the SBC would ever adopt a "moderately narrow theology,"[8] the theology that Rogers believed the SBC began with in 1845. In the same interview Rogers said that Southern Baptists had "made a golden calf" out of the Cooperative Program, by which he meant the entire work of the denomination. This last statement aroused so much ire that Rogers took the platform at the Southern Baptist Convention in New Orleans in June to issue a word of explanation and apology.

In addition to Rogers's "golden calf" statement, Fundamentalists committed other major gaffes that under normal circumstances would have sabotaged their cause. Paul Pressler registered for the meeting of the SBC in Houston in 1979 as a messenger of a church of which he was not a member, clearly a violation of the SBC constitution. Wayne Dehoney, a former president of the SBC, took the SBC platform, waved at the sky boxes where Pressler and Patterson were sitting, and verbally eviscerated Pressler for his unethical registration. Additionally, in the spring of 1980 Paige Patterson created a backlash when he called the names of seven Southern Baptists, some of whom were quite popular, who represented for him the nature and extent of liberalism in Southern Baptist life. Fundamentalists always fared better with general accusations than with specific name-calling.

In August of 1980, after he had been elected SBC president in June, Bailey Smith, one of the more unguarded but colorful of the Fundamentalists, created something of a national religious furor when he said that "God Almighty does not hear the prayer of a Jew." Moderates, wondering where this left Jesus, showcased this sentence for what it was: authentic fundamentalist intolerance. The very next month, Paul Pressler announced to a group of Baptists in Virginia that the Fundamentalists "need to go for the jugular—we need to go for the trustees," by which he meant the domination of the SBC. His language left little to the imagination as to the fundamentalist agenda, although such agenda was then and has continued to be denied.

One can point to other signs of uncertainty of a fundamentalist victory in these early years. During two of the four years from 1980–1983, two "unaligned" preachers were elected to the coveted position of president of the SBC Pastor's Conference. These were Jim Henry and Ed Young, both of whom had not yet identified with the fundamentalist movement. Later, however, as the Pressler-Patterson movement picked up steam, Henry would endorse the fundamentalist cause and Young would join it outright. The other two presidents of the Pastor's Conference during this period were Fred Wolfe and Charles Stanley, unequivocating Fundamentalists. The point is, however, that the Fundamentalists were not yet at the swaggering stage, winning everything up for vote.

Moderates, moreover, had enough victories in the early years to offer some encouragement to their side. At the 1979 SBC meeting where Dehoney publicly embarrassed Pressler, Moderates also adopted a resolution in appreciation of their seminaries, defeated a constitutional amendment that would have prevented ordained women from serving on the home or foreign mission field, and reaffirmed a restrained 1976 resolution on abortion. Five years later such action would be unheard of.

What appeared to some as a major moderate victory in 1981 turned out not to be so. Herschel H. Hobbs, former SBC president, primary author of the 1963 SBC confessional statement, and the nearest person to a "pope" Southern Baptists had at the time, tried to squash the inerrancy brouhaha with a motion that missed its mark. At the Los Angeles convention Hobbs called upon the SBC to reaffirm its 1963 confessional statement, including the preface, which, as Hobbs said, "protects the individual and guards us from a creedal faith." The apparent intent of the motion was to reaffirm the non-creedal and voluntary nature of the confessional statement while appeasing the fundamentalist insistence on inerrancy.

Moderates were slow learners. One does not appease Fundamentalists. During later debate on the motion, Adrian Rogers deftly requested that some of Hobbs's comments that reflected the inerrantist tendency be read into the record. Later in the controversy, Hobbs's comments would be cited by Fundamentalists as case history that "The Baptist Faith and Message" article on the Bible was an inerrantist statement. Fundamentalists used Hobbs's statements that "leaned" toward inerrancy to better effect than Moderates used Hobbs's statement about the noncreedal and voluntary nature of "The Baptist Faith and Message." Again, however, in 1981 many people erroneously thought that Hobbs's effort at peacekeeping would do the trick for Moderates, but it did not.

In this earliest phase of the struggle, almost every Baptist state editor editorialized against the Fundamentalists, while the denominational bureaucracy was solidly but silently against the Patterson-Pressler efforts. If you add to this the early fundamentalist goofs and the not unimpressive moderate victories recounted above, you may wonder why things turned out as they did. Do not forget that Fundamentalists experienced enough victories in these early years to keep them charging, even if cautiously and while taking a step back every now and then. They impressively won every year the SBC presidency, with the enormous appointive powers for implementing the inerrancy strategy. Moreover, they kept control of the Pastor's Conference, more or less.

In 1980 Fundamentalists successfully presented and persuaded the SBC to adopt a resolution entitled "On Doctrinal Integrity." That resolution admonished SBC trustees to only employ, and continue the employment of, faculty members and professional staff who believe in the divine inspiration of the whole Bible, infallibility of the original manuscripts, and the Bible is truth without any error.

Again in 1981, fundamentalist power defeated a moderate motion that would have limited the appointive powers of the SBC president, the control button in the convention. In 1982 SBC resolutions engineered by Fundamentalists endorsed scientific creationism, a federal constitutional amendment prohibiting abortion, and an amendment regarding voluntary prayer in public schools. These resolutions marked a deviation from past SBC actions regarding government involvement in religious matters and indicated a clear turn to the right in SBC life. Fundamentalists landed some huge blows in the first phase of the conflict.

Forced to select a single event in these early years that profiled the future conflict within the SBC, one would do well to point to the 1979 SBC Pastor's Conference in Houston. The name could be misleading. It is a "preaching conference," a preaching conference for pastors that meets immediately prior to the annual meeting of the SBC. In the decade of the controversy, it became an orchestrated political rally for SBC fundamentalism. Bill Leonard was correct when he said that "1979 was the culmination of a century of doctrinal debate and the beginning of a new denominational coalition."[9] That new denominational coalition's first public manifestation, however, appeared at the Pastor's Conference in Houston in 1979.

The SBC Pastor's Conference that year contained three ingredients of the future fundamentalist agenda. The first was the denominational agenda of control reflected not only in the pre-convention politicking of Patterson and Pressler, but also in the announcement of Criswell that Baptists had gathered to elect Rogers as SBC president and in the vitriolic sermon of evangelist James Robison. Robison said,

> I believe we must not only elect a president who believes the Bible is the infallible, inerrant word of the living God, but we must elect a president who is totally committed to the removal from this denomination of any teacher, any educator who does not believe the Bible is the infallible, inerrant word of the living God."[10]

The entire fundamentalist worldview, including the inerrancy formula, would be used in the future to purge SBC institutions of non-fundamentalist leaders and transform the SBC.

Second, the theological agenda of inerrancy constituted a major thrust of sermons at the Pastor's Conference, especially those by Robison and Adrian Rogers. With broad swipes at "liberals," "humanists," entrenched denominational bureaucrats, and professors caricatured by Robison as "walking corpses," Rogers and Robison brought the vast majority of the audience to its feet again and again.

Third, the national agenda of right-wing politics became explicit in Charles Stanley's Pastor's Conference sermon "Stand Up America." While never alluding to Jerry Falwell or his "Moral Majority" movement, Stanley's sermon called upon Southern Baptist preachers and laity to unite with this extremist ideology.

The entire fundamentalist agenda came packaged in passionate, incendiary, and inflammatory preaching. Preachers became provocateurs, fomenters of dissatisfaction with what was going on both within the denomination and the nation. Anyone who doubts the power of the pulpit to bring about radical change should revisit the tapes of SBC fundamentalist preachers during the decade of the 1980s. The political organizing of Pressler and Patterson, left to itself, would have never changed the SBC. Without the bombastic rhetoric of Rogers and Stanley and other preachers like them at national SBC gatherings, the fundamentalist political machine may have still been on the runway. Because of that rhetoric, however, the take-off occurred at Houston in 1979.[11]

Phase Two: 1984–1987

The period of 1984–1987 marked a decisive momentum swing toward the Fundamentalists. Some signs of this swing existed at the 1983 SBC meeting in Pittsburgh, though it was one of the calmest conventions during the entire controversy. Amidst the apparent Pittsburgh tranquility, James Draper, the third successive Fundamentalist to be elected SBC president, went unopposed by the Moderates for a second-year term. Deciding not to challenge Draper, Moderates then unsuccessfully challenged nominations of the fundamentalist-stacked Committee on Boards. This was the first failure of the Moderates at modifying the nominations of this powerful board.

Also amidst the Pittsburgh calm, Fundamentalists displayed Charles
Stanley for one of his first major appearances at a meeting of the Southern Baptist Convention. Elected president of the SBC Pastor's Conference
prior to the Pittsburgh convention, Stanley, the popular television preacher and pastor of First Baptist Church, Atlanta, Georgia, also gained
platform time as chair of the powerful Committee on Boards. Elected president of the SBC the next year, Stanley was crucial for the fundamentalist
machine during the years of the fiercest struggle of the controversy.

Many interpreters have seen the 1985 SBC in Dallas as the single
most important turning point in the conflict. Others thought it came a
year later in Atlanta in 1986. Both Dallas and Atlanta loomed huge in the
outcome of the controversy. The momentum swing, however, that pushed
the Fundamentalists to eventual victory came, in my judgment, a year
earlier in 1984 in Kansas City.

What happened in Kansas City that was so telling for the future? Two
elections. In that year Southern Baptists spoke volumes about the change
they were undergoing when they elected as their president a person who
had been, until the previous year, on the very margin of Southern Baptist
life. Messengers to the 1984 SBC elected Charles Stanley on the first
ballot over John Sullivan, a nonaligned Shreveport pastor, and Grady
Cothen, a man of impeccable denominational service. Cothen had served
Southern Baptists faithfully for decades as a popular preacher, a local
church pastor, a state convention executive, the president of a Baptist
college, the president of a Baptist seminary, and most recently as president of the Baptist Sunday School Board. For messengers to reject Grady
Cothen, a staunch biblical Conservative and devoted denominationalist,
for Charles Stanley, a biblical Fundamentalist and marginal Southern
Baptist, meant that Fundamentalists had been enormously successful in
heralding the fundamentalist program as the new badge of denominational
identity.

The messengers went further, however. They elected Paul Pressler,
one of the two architects of the fundamentalist takeover of the convention, to a crucial position on the SBC Executive Committee. Pressler had
been viewed by many elements of the conflict as one of the genuine
extremists among Fundamentalists. While Moderates challenged his election, Pressler's accession to the most powerful committee in Southern
Baptist life marked the legitimation of theological and political extremism
within the denomination unprecedented in Southern Baptist history. If

absolutely nothing else had happened in Kansas City, the elections of Stanley as president and Pressler to the SBC Executive Committee suggested that "school was almost out" for the Moderates and the SBC as it had been known.

The Kansas City convention was also a defining moment for women in the future SBC. By a vote of 58% to 42% messengers adopted a hotly debated resolution entitled "On Ordination and the Role of Women in Ministry." Accenting their hierarchical understanding of the world and a clearly submissive role of women to men, Fundamentalists announced that

> while Paul commends women and men alike in other roles of ministry and service (Titus 2:1-10), he excludes women from pastoral leadership (1 Tim 2:12) to preserve a submission God requires because the man was first in creation and the woman was first in the Edenic fall (1 Tim 2:13ff).

Moderates saw the resolution as antithetical to the spirit of Jesus, abusive of women, and an example of biblical and theological interpretation used to reinforce unbridled male egos and sinful self-centeredness. No issue in the controversy more starkly contrasts the fundamentalist and moderate approach to Scripture than does the role of women in the church. Using Galatians 3:27-28 where Paul says, "There is no longer Jew or Greek, there is no longer slave or fee, there is no longer male and female; for all of you are one in Christ Jesus," Moderates countered the fundamentalist prooftexting with some of their own. In a 1991 public document designed to distinguish moderate from fundamentalist Southern Baptists, Moderates declared,

> We take Galatians as a clue to the way the church should be ordered. We interpret the reference to women the same way we interpret the reference to slaves. If we have submissive roles for women, we must also have a place for the slaves in the church.
>
> In Galatians Paul follows the spirit of Jesus who courageously challenged the conventional wisdom of his day. It was a wisdom with rigid boundaries between men and women in religion and in public life. Jesus deliberately broke those barriers. He called women to follow him; he treated women as equally capable of dealing with sacred issues. Our model for the role of women in matters of faith is the Lord Jesus." [12]

Despite a powerful rebuke of the attitudes and efforts of Fundamentalists from Southwestern Seminary president Russell Dilday in his SBC sermon at Kansas City, Fundamentalists won every major vote in 1984. Moderates managed to derail their adversaries' effort to defund the Baptist Joint Committee on Public Affairs, but that was the best they could do. It was their lone victory in Kansas City. Moderate defeat at the 1984 SBC, however, never meant acquiescence.

Following Kansas City, denominational agency heads, especially seminary presidents Russell Dilday of Southwestern, Randall Lolley of Southeastern, and Roy Honeycutt of Southern, entered the fray in a public way, flailing away. They and others worked indescribably hard, but it was too little, too late. Even though the 1985 and 1986 SBCs in Dallas and Atlanta hosted the largest crowds in SBC history, and even though Moderates showcased their most electable presidential candidate in Winfred Moore for both years, they could not muster the necessary votes to win the presidency.

The turning point was at Kansas City, not Dallas or Atlanta. Referring to the so-called "Shootout in Dallas" in 1985, Paige Patterson said,

> Our hearts had been in our mouth every year up until Dallas but coming off the victory in Kansas City we had more confidence than ever before. By then we knew how to communicate effectively.[13]

He understated the situation. At Kansas City his group had learned more than how to communicate effectively; they had learned to win impressively with some of their most extreme people.

If Fundamentalists delivered a decisive blow in Kansas City in 1984, knockdowns of Moderates came in rapid succession at annual meetings of the SBC.

—In Dallas, 1985, Stanley was reelected president over Winfred Moore by a margin of 55.3% to 44.7%, and a "Peace Committee" was appointed that would be adroitly used to further SBC fundamentalism.

—In Atlanta, 1986, Adrian Rogers was elected president over Winfred Moore by a margin of 54.22% to 45.78%, and a bylaw amendment was adopted that guaranteed the appointive powers of the president and fundamentalist control.

—In St. Louis, 1987, Adrian Rogers was reelected president over Richard Jackson by a vote of 59.97% to 40.03%; and the Peace Committee Report was accepted, a major triumph for the right wing of the SBC.

With the election of the fundamentalist presidential candidates at these three conventions, the Pressler-Patterson coalition tightened its grip on the SBC political machine and increasingly attracted the previously fence-sitting pastors to the side of power and triumph.

Not only were Fundamentalists winning; some denominational leaders began capitulating to the steamroller. In many ways the single most demoralizing event for the moderate cause came on 22 October 1986, in Glorieta, New Mexico. On that day the seminary presidents presented to the SBC Peace Committee what came to be known as "The Glorieta Statement." While some seminary presidents, especially Lolley, Dilday, and Honeycutt, were broadly perceived as among the staunchest opponents to the takeover, "The Glorieta Statement" constituted little less than a theological surrender to fundamentalism, especially to its language about the Bible.

"The sixty-six books of the Bible," said the seminary presidents, "are not errant in any area of reality." Nothing could have pleased Adrian Rogers more. Moderates and Fundamentalists both saw this as nails in the moderate coffin. Later some of the presidents would seek to "clarify" and "explain" and even back away from that statement, but the damage was done. Cecil Sherman, the most militant moderate voice on the Peace Committee, resigned in protest and despair. Later he wrote that

> The Glorieta Statement was shameful. It was not the truth, and the people who wrote the statement knew it. The presidents said what they thought they had to say to "save" their schools, but in so doing, they gutted serious theological education among Southern Baptists for at least a generation. Well-placed people will deny my assessment of the effects of the Glorieta Statement, but the exodus of good teachers from our seminaries, the rape of Southeastern Seminary, the exodus of top-notch faculty members . . . from Southern Seminary and the resulting transformation of that historic school, and the climate of fear and intimidation that now exists at places that once were free makes my point.[14]

Unfortunately, subsequent events at Southeastern where both President Lolley and Dean Ashcraft resigned, at Southwestern with the gestapo-like firing of Russell Dilday as president in March 1994, and the horrendously tyrannical actions at Southern Seminary by fundamentalist president Al Mohler in 1994 and 1995 proved Cecil Sherman right. Mohler forced out Molly Marshall, a tenured female theologian, fired Diana Garland as dean of the School of Social Work, and effectively gagged his faculty members and gutted their freedom. At Glorieta the seminary presidents made the mistake that many Southern Baptists made during the fight: they thought one might be able to negotiate with non-negotiating Fundamentalists. Not so.

Phase Three: 1988–1990

Despite the thriving momentum of the right-wing of the denomination, Moderates would not quit—not yet, at least. Conditions had gotten so bad for them, however, that W. A. Criswell could savagely and publicly malign them as "skunks" in his 1988 Pastor's Conference address. Nonetheless, Moderates made their best showing in the presidential election at San Antonio in 1988. Jerry Vines, the fundamentalist candidate, beat Richard Jackson, the moderate candidate, by a razor thin vote of 15,804 to 15,112, a margin of 692 and a percentage of 50.53% to 48.32%.

Fundamentalists would often claim that 95% of Southern Baptists agreed with them on the issues. The presidential elections, the best barometer of the divided Southern Baptist house, belied this claim. When non-incumbents competed for the presidency during the decade long controversy, Fundamentalists won by the following margins: 1979, 51.36%; 1980, 51.67%; 1982, 56.97%; 1984, 52.18%; 1986, 54.22%; 1988, 50.53%; 1990, 57.68%. Impressive to be sure, but the nearest thing to a rout came in the final year of the conflict and this with Fundamentalists' weakest candidate for the decade, demonstrating only that fundamentalist momentum mushroomed by 1990. For Fundamentalists to claim 95% of the SBC family at least proves that their mathematics were not inerrant!

With newly discovered might Fundamentalists took bold steps to solidify their power, even to the point of revising the Baptist heritage. At the 1988 meeting of the SBC in San Antonio, messengers adopted a resolution that virtually de-baptistified the SBC. Known as "On the Priesthood of the Believer," it was presented by and voted for by people who simply did not know the Baptist heritage. The resolution actually diminished and perverted the historic Baptist principle of the priesthood of all believers, misrepresented Baptist theologians who had written on the subject, falsified the position of the "Baptist Faith and Message" on the topic, and non-baptistically exalted the authority of the pastor.[15] And it passed by a 54.75% majority! No wonder that Randall Lolley led a group of Moderates from the convention center to the Alamo and ceremonially tore up that resolution! "Resolution 5" did not represent anything in the Baptist heritage.

As a result of Bill Moyers's December 1987 PBS documentary entitled "God and Politics," Daniel Vestal, pastor of First Baptist Church, Midland, Texas, emerged to the forefront of the moderate movement. He challenged Vines for the SBC presidency at Las Vegas in 1989, garnering an impressive 43.39% of the votes against an incumbent president. It was not enough, however. At New Orleans the next year, 1990, Vestal went head to head with Morris Chapman, fundamentalist pastor of First Baptist Church, Wichita Falls, Texas, and was soundly defeated by Chapman 57.68% to 42.32%.

After New Orleans, Moderates were exhausted by their decade of losing. They quit the politics of the SBC. They continued, however, a process that they had begun as early as 1983, creating their own structures. In historical order Moderates created *Baptists Today* (April 1983), Southern Baptist Women in Ministry (June 1983), the Forum (June 1984), the Southern Baptist Alliance (December 1986), Baptists Committed (December 1988), the Associated Baptist Press (July 1990), Baptist Cooperative Missions Program, Inc. (August 1990), the Cooperative Baptist Fellowship (August 1990), Smyth and Helwys Publishing, Inc. (November 1990), the Baptist Center for Ethics (May 1991), the Baptist Theological Seminary at Richmond (September 1991), and the William H. Whitsitt Baptist Heritage Society (October 1992). The Cooperative Baptist Fellowship, called into being by Daniel Vestal in 1990, is the glue that holds the moderate movement together.

On the other side of the SBC aisle, Fundamentalists had captured by August 1986 the balance of power on the first SBC agency board of trustees. After that the "domino theory" came into operation. One agency after another came under the domination of aggressive proteges of Rogers, Patterson, and Pressler. With a majority on the boards of trustees, Fundamentalists began electing their denominational agency heads: Larry Lewis at the Home Mission Board (April 1987), Lewis Drummond at Southeastern Seminary (March 1988), Richard Land at the Christian Life Commission (September 1988), James Draper at the Baptist Sunday

School Board (July 1991), Morris Chapman at the Executive Committee (February 1992), Paige Patterson at Southeastern to replace Drummond (May 1992), Al Mohler at Southern Seminary (1993), and by the end of 1995 the fundamentalist lock on the denomination will be virtually complete.

III

After both living through the controversy and studying its remains, I have a hunch that Fundamentalists got far more than they ever expected. Surely it was not more than they wanted. Their actions have clearly demonstrated what they wanted: absolute control of a denomination that biblically, theologically, ethically, and politically reflects their fundamentalist view of the world. But I seriously doubt that even Pressler or Patterson anticipated in 1979 getting absolute control of the denomination. Moreover, while it was a gargantuan struggle, my guess is that in the end it was far easier than Fundamentalists would have ever imagined.

Why and how did they win? Fundamentalism had never been able to capture the conservative SBC before. Why during the 1980s? By now many answers—wise and unwise—have been given. One simple answer, of course, is that God willed it. Paige Patterson, not surprisingly, has used this interpretation. The controversy was not only "right," but "the commandment of God." [16] Patterson himself, however, stops short of saying that either "winning" or "losing" are necessarily signs of God's will. Some of his colleagues were not as careful.

Another simplistic explanation is more pragmatic. Fundamentalists persuaded more messengers to attend the annual conventions and vote for their presidential candidate than did the Moderates. Based on sheer numbers of people voting, it is now easy to say, "Moderates could never have won." As a matter of fact, SBC history itself contradicts that. While no such thing as "Moderates" existed before 1980, traditional Southern Baptists, the ancestors of Moderates, had always successfully resisted extremism such as J. R. Graves's Landmarkism and Frank Norris's fundamentalism.

More to the question at hand is why traditional Southern Baptists were unsuccessful in the 1980s. While many other factors may have been important, I suggest Fundamentalists won because of these factors: emotional passion, theological clarity, cultural congruity, organizational unity, and personal leadership.

Emotional Passion

The power of emotional passion should be most instructive to other denominations that are threatened by extremists of whatever kind. James Slatton, a passionate Moderate, said, "We always worked with the disadvantage that Moderates were, by definition, *moderate.*" He meant that passion won and moderation lost. Cecil Sherman echoed Slatton even more passionately:

> Moderates did not have enough moral energy to win. We could not bring ourselves to use moral language to describe our cause. Truth was butchered. We said nothing. Good people were defamed. We were silent. Baptist principles were mangled and Baptist history was replaced, rewritten. All the while, teachers who could have written about the problems in calling the Bible inerrant, did not. And preachers who could have called us to arms, said nothing. The want of moral energy was the undoing of the moderate movement.[17]

Samuel Hill, the leading interpreter of religion in the American South, has a helpful analysis of southern evangelical Protestantism that is applicable at this point. Hill lists four types of evangelicalism in the South: (1) the truth oriented, rightly called "fundamentalist"; (2) the conversion oriented who are "evangelistic"; (3) the spiritually oriented, "devotional" in nature; and (4) the service oriented, "ethical" in nature and concerned with justice issues.[18] While one may find all four types in a single denomination and certainly in the old SBC, one should also note a very significant attitudinal difference among the four types. Types 2, 3, and 4 tend to be inclusive, relational, and non-absolutist. Type 1, the truth oriented, tends to be exclusive, rationalistic, and dogmatic.

It is a descriptive, not a derogatory, statement to say that this is the very nature of the type of fundamentalism that captured the Southern Baptist Convention. When a Christian believes that he or she has a monopoly on the gospel and others err because they do not agree with a certain interpretation, trust is out the window, reconciliation is impossible, and Christians with a different point of view are labeled dangerous and heretical. The uncompromising, non-negotiating aspect of fundamentalism can only be understood in light of the passionate conviction that Ffundamentalists and Fundamentalists alone are the truth-people. They think they *are* being "fair" when they do not appoint people to committees who disagree with them. They think they *are* being "fair" when they want people fired from faculties who do not agree with them. They think they *are* being "fair" when they want only their kind appointed to positions of leadership in the denomination.

Some among them, to be sure, are simply small and petulant persons. We all have names of people who fall into this category. Fundamentalists are not alone in this moral shortfall, however. On the other hand, I would argue that some of them are people of conscience. More convicted by a particular understanding of truth than they are mean in spirit, their passionate and unbending and inflexible understanding of truth makes them appear mean in spirit. Their understanding of truth simply must exclude rather than include because for them truth is more important than love, a point that most Moderates think the Fundamentalists would have trouble reconciling with Jesus' understanding of authentic religious faith. It should come as no surprise that the multi-volume, celebrated fundamentalist interpretation of the controversy is entitled *The Truth in Crisis*. Actually, Christian "truth" was never at risk, unless by the Fundamentalists themselves.

Theological Clarity

Extremism of whatever kind rides to the front of the parade pontificating shibboleths, simplistic slogans, and watchwords. "Inerrancy" as it relates to the Bible is such a word, and most of fundamentalist scholarship knows this. Push Fundamentalists hard and they will qualify it nine different ways. But "bumper sticker theology" that is brief, unambiguous, and passionate communicates. It even intimidates.

Moderates got tongue-tied in their non-responses to the theological oversimplifications of fundamentalism. Fundamentalists spoke in spades; Moderates could not speak in spades. They honestly knew the subject was too knotty and ambiguous for that kind of sleight of the theological hand. To say that one reads the Bible, studies the Bible, tries to live by the Bible, and loves the Bible was not enough for inerrantist Fundamentalists. Moderates did not say soon enough or loudly enough or simply enough what Cecil Sherman wrote in italics: *"Inerrancy is not the truth."* In their address to the public in 1990, the interim steering committee members of the Cooperative Baptist Fellowship asserted that "the Bible neither claims nor reveals inerrancy as a Christian teaching." That candor early in the controversy would have been a better offense for Moderates than always being forced into theological defensiveness.

Cultural Congruity

By the 1980s America, indeed the world, appeared to be moving away from toleration. Just as Islamic fundamentalism gained power throughout the world, Christian fundamentalism ascended in America. Jerry Falwell, Jim Bakker, Jimmy Swaggart, Charles Stanley, Oral Roberts, and a host of other television preachers bombarded the nation's airways and for the most part went unchallenged by mainstream American religion. This trend only reinforced the swing to the right wing in Southern Baptist life.

Of course, what was happening religiously was happening also in national politics. Carter was out; Reagan was coming in. When Bailey Smith made his statement that "God Almighty does not hear the prayer of a Jew," he was on the platform with several other past or future Southern Baptist Convention presidents. Together, they and other leaders of the religious right listened and applauded when Ronald Reagan addressed some 20,000 participants. Reagan's election reflected and strengthened the fundamentalist ascendancy within the SBC. The extremist movement within Southern Baptist life in the 1980s had a stronger ally in the culture than any previous controversy in the denomination. Moderates, on the other hand, were constantly swimming upstream.

Organizational Unity

Understandably, Moderates never had the apparent lock-step unanimity that Fundamentalists had. Moderates do not think as militarily. When a group of the fundamentalist leaders began to lead some cruises together, they facetiously were dubbed by Moderates as the "Caribbean Cardinals." As Sherman pointed out, however, a cruise ship was not necessary to transport the fundamentalist decision-makers. Sherman said they could have ridden in a minivan. I think they could have been comfortable in a pickup truck if it did not have bucket seats. By the middle of the decade they needed room for only three—Rogers, Patterson, and Pressler—and Rogers was driving.

While Cecil Sherman was the single most important, consistent, and clearest moderate voice throughout the decade, not all Moderates followed him the way Fundamentalists followed Rogers. At one point he relinquished the leadership to Don Harbuck, then James Slatton, then John Jeffers. At another point Foy Valentine was responsible for "getting out the vote," and for a brief period the seminary presidents led the moderate procession.

Personal Leadership

While the personal leadership factor is closely connected to the issue of organizational unity, they are not necessarily the same. Thus far in most of the interpretations explaining why the controversy turned out as it did, too little attention has been given to the dimension of personal leadership.

Often overlooked is the fact that the SBC was in a "generational crease" immediately prior to and in the early years of the controversy. Southern Baptists had a changing of the guard in many of its agencies and institutions as well as in some of the larger pulpits in SBC life. In the evolution controversy of the 1920s the denomination solidified around E. Y. Mullins, while in the turbulent 1960s Herschel H. Hobbs commanded a hearing. During the fundamentalist-moderate conflict Porter Routh, Baker James Cauthen, James Sullivan, Duke McCall, Grady Cothen, and Albert McClellan—all prominent denominational leaders—retired within a matter of a few years of each other, either immediately before or in the early years of the epic struggle. Naturally, those who replaced them did not have comparable influence in the denomination. When Moderates called upon some of these revered leaders—McCall and Cothen, especially—who had given their lives to the SBC, they were disdainfully dismissed by the Fundamentalists as being part of the problem.

If one generation was passing off the scene, much of the rising generation of traditional Baptists on the scene chose silence over confrontation. In his recent book *The New SBC*, Grady Cothen bemoans the deafening silence from the multitudes in the SBC regarding the new fundamentalism, and then releases two paragraphs that blister denominational leadership from directors of missions to presidents of national agencies—

including all the college presidents, state executive directors, and state denominational employees in between. In addition, Cothen notes that many pastors did not educate their members about the problems and/or blindly held to the view that the controversy did not affect them.[19] A part of the story of this controversy had to do with the absence of the courage to resist.

In Sherman, Slatton, Chafin, Vestal, and others, Moderates had courageous and convicted leadership, but apparently Fundamentalists had even more of that kind. In compliment rather than criticism, someone said that Pressler and Patterson were theological pit bulldogs. Charles Stanley had a national audience by virtue of television ministry. W. A. Criswell probably does not deserve as much credit for the triumph of the new fundamentalism as history will grant him, but he certainly was the granddaddy of the movement. While I do not subscribe to a simple and singular biographical view of history, I sincerely doubt that fundamentalism could have known its measure of success apart from Adrian Rogers. Three times the president of the SBC in a span of nine years, he was crucial in the pro-fundamentalist outcome of the Peace Committee. No other Fundamentalist could rival him as preacher, debater, or intransigent believer.

IV

What have been the results of the Fundamentalist-Moderate Controversy for the SBC? William Stone said in his study that the conflict "redefined Southern Baptists, revised their history, remythologized their future, and reformed their values, beliefs, and social relationships."[20] Grady Cothen, a man who knows the SBC inside out, said,

> Whatever else can be said about the SBC, it is no longer the same body in doctrine, polity, procedures, or cooperative effort in education and missions.[21]

Stone, Cothen, and other interpreters confirm my earlier assertion that the controversy changed almost everything in SBC life.

Space precludes a description of all the changes in the SBC brought about by the new fundamentalist leaders and their triumph. These changes are yet in process, so the final story cannot be told. To this point, however, the following summary is clear: theologically and ideologically the SBC has been *fundamentalized*; ecclesiologically the SBC has been *centralized*; culturally, in terms of gender issues, the SBC has been *chauvinized*; ecumenically the SBC has been *sectarianized*; denominationally the SBC has been *de-baptistified*.

Theologically and ideologically, the new SBC has been fundamentalized. For years the SBC was a "conservative" denomination. While the present fundamentalist leaders want to maintain the "conservative" terminology and apply it to themselves, they have great difficulty doing this because the difference between them and the old conservative leadership is so radically stark. Pressler, Patterson, Rogers, and Stanley are much closer to independent fundamentalist Jerry Falwell than they are to traditional Southern Baptists such as George W. Truett, E. Y. Mullins, Baker James Cauthen, or even Herschel H. Hobbs. Certainly this does not mean that all Southern Baptists are now Fundamentalists, but increasingly non-fundamentalist persons within the SBC will have problems establishing an identity apart from the powerful new leadership.

Basic to the fundamentalizing of the SBC is the theological constrictionism, the narrowing theology that expresses itself in creedalism. Baptists of the South organized the SBC in 1845, so 1995 marks the 150th anniversary of the convention. At the first meeting of the SBC in Augusta in 1845, messengers claimed that they had no creed but the Bible. By 1995, however, that disclaimer, while yet a part of denominational rhetoric, has been effectively shelved.

The SBC has become a creedalistic structure. This is a charge the Fundamentalists bristle at and deny, because they know they have stepped outside the Baptist heritage. While eschewing the word "creeds," they now speak of doctrinal "parameters." Their public statements and actions, however, support the assessment that the SBC is increasingly creedal. In the interest of integrity and clarity, the fundamentalist leadership would be better served to state this publicly. In addition to the 1963 "Statement of the Baptist Faith and Message," Fundamentalists now call for compliance to the "Glorieta Statement," the "Peace Committee Report," "The Chicago Statement on Biblical Inerrancy," and the resolutions and motions adopted at annual meetings of the SBC.

Ecclesiologically, the SBC has become centralized. Increasingly, the term "The Southern Baptist Church" appears in letters to the editor. While that term represents a gross misinterpretation of the Baptist doctrine of the church, it reflects many developments in Southern Baptist life since 1979. Historically, resolutions adopted at the annual sessions were never considered "denominational law" for SBC agencies and institutions. Since 1979 such resolutions have increasingly been interpreted as "directives," centralizing all agencies around SBC actions. In June 1994, administrators at Southern Seminary told Professor Molly Marshall that she should resign or suffer the possibility of dismissal from her position on the faculty. The vice president for academic affairs indicated that her alleged disregard for the content of motions and resolutions passed at the SBC constituted one of the possible charges against her.

SBC constitutional changes, SBC actions that in effect deny the liberty of the local churches to channel funds according to the church's desires, legislative actions of the SBC Executive Committee toward individual SBC agencies, and intrusions by SBC agencies into state convention life are further examples of a growing centralization in the Southern Baptist Convention.[22] A new federalism accompanies the new fundamentalism in SBC life. Just as constrictionism is at work in matters of theology, centripetal forces are operative in the denominational machinery. Voices that began bemoaning "denominational bureaucracy" end up intensifying it. The present centralization process within the SBC substantiates the early moderate contention that "control" was a major feature of the controversy.

Culturally, in terms of gender equality, the SBC has become chauvinized by its male fundamentalist leadership. Since its adoption in 1984, the Kansas City resolution has been used as case law in SBC agencies. Not only has male "headship" been affirmed by Fundamentalists, but women, so the new SBC leadership contend, have no role as deacons or pastors in a local church. When new seminary president Ken Hemphill of Southwestern Seminary announced the addition of a woman to the faculty of the theology school, he noted that she would be teaching only church history and not theology, and he also assured the SBC constituency that she was "under" the authority of the seminary president at work and her husband at home. At Southern Seminary in Louisville, Kentucky, Al Mohler, fundamentalist president, announced in April 1995 a litmus test for hiring faculty that included opposition to women serving as pastors.

Ecumenically, the fundamentalist leadership has sectarianized the Southern Baptist Convention. Long before 1979 and the rise of the new fundamentalism in SBC life, ecumenists viewed the SBC as one of the major problem children of American Protestantism. One of the results of the controversy, however, is that the SBC has been taken further out of the mainstream of American Christianity, increasingly relating itself to the radical right wing followers of American Protestantism. This sectarianism is expressed not only in the groups with which they associate, but with the Baptist groups, such as the Cooperative Baptist Fellowship, that they have repudiated.

Denominationally, the new fundamentalism has de-baptistified the SBC. Examples are abundant: the growing creedalism, the novel emphasis on pastoral authority and the corresponding diminishing of the priesthood of all believers and congregational church government, and the incredible notion of W. A. Criswell that the separation of church and state was the figment of some infidel's imagination. This debaptistification of the SBC is obviously something that the new SBC leadership denies. One would not be surprised, however, if William Brackney, a non-Southern Baptist historian, was thinking of the new SBC when he said of Baptists today:

> They have strayed from their beginnings. The loudest and most obvious and most often quoted Baptists in the United States seem to be nowhere near the historic principles of older Baptist bodies."[23]

Notes

[1]In this chapter I draw from my previously published works on this subject, especially "A Chronology," "Introduction," and "The Struggle for the Soul of the SBC: Reflections and Interpretations," in *The Struggle for the Soul of the SBC: Moderate Responses to the Fundamentalist Movement*, Walter B. Shurden, ed. (Macon GA: Mercer University Press, 1993) ix-xviii, xix-xxvii, 275-90; "Inerrancy Controversy, SBC," in *Dictionary of Baptists in America*, Bill J. Leonard, ed. (Downers Grove IL: InterVarsity Press, 1994) 151-52; "Major Issues in the SBC Controversy," in *Amidst Babel, Speak the Truth*, Robert U. Ferguson, Jr., ed. (Macon GA: Smyth & Helwys, 1993) 1-10; "The Southern Baptist Synthesis: Is It Cracking?" and "The Inerrancy Debate: A Comparative Study of Southern Baptist Controversies," *Baptist History and Heritage* 16/2 (April 1981): 2-19.

[2]For these percentages see my "Chronology" in *The Struggle for the Soul of the SBC*.

[3]Diane Winston, "The Southern Baptist Story," in *Southern Baptists Observed: Multiple Perspectives on a Changing Denomination*, Nancy Tatom Ammerman, ed. (Knoxville TN: University of Tennessee Press, 1993) 17-18.

[4]Ibid., 18.

[5]While maintaining no mistakes in the original autographs of the Bible, Patterson said that grammatical mistakes and "transcribal inadvertencies" exist so that "we can now arrive at a 98-percent accurate text." See "Patterson Group Seeks Long Range Control of

SBC," Baptist Press, 21 April 1980, 4. Pressler also spoke of "a few scribal errors which do not affect any doctrine." See "An Interview with Judge Paul Pressler," *The Controversy in the Southern Baptist Convention* (this was a special issue of *The Theological Educator*, a magazine published semiannually by the faculty of the New Orleans Baptist Theological Seminary) 1985, 22.

[6]See, for example, James Carl Hefley, *The Truth in Crisis*, (Dallas: Criterion Publications, 1986). Hefley's work may be considered the "official" fundamentalist interpretation of the conflict, and he published four subsequent volumes under the same general title with different publishers. See also, Joe Edward Barnhart, *The Southern Baptist Holy War* (Austin TX: Texas Monthly Press, 1986), a very important book for understanding the philosophical and theological dimensions of the conflict. Ellen M. Rosenberg, *The Southern Baptists: A Subculture in Transition* (Knoxville: University of Tennessee Press, 1989), a narrowly sociological interpretation of the conflict that nevertheless contains important insights. Claude L. Howe, Jr., "From Houston to Dallas: Recent Controversy in the Southern Baptist Convention," and "From Dallas to New Orleans: The Controversy Continues," *The Theological Educator* (Spring 1990), an excellent year-by-year chronological portrayal of the controversy, and would be one of the best with which to begin a study of the struggle. Nancy Tatom Ammerman, *Baptist Battles* (New Brunswick NJ: Rutgers University Press, 1990), a very important work, heavily cultural and sociological in approach, written by a Moderate but praised by fundamentalist Paige Patterson. Bill J. Leonard, *God's Last and Only Hope* (Grand Rapids MI: Eerdmans, 1990), one of the best overall treatments of the controversy in book form. Ralph H. Elliott, *The Genesis Controversy and Continuity in Southern Baptist Chaos: A Eulogy for a Great Tradition* (Macon GA: Mercer University Press, 1992), a blistering indictment of what he calls SBC "doublespeak" and a very important book for understanding previous controversies as antecedent to the Fundamentalist-Moderate Controversy. Grady C. Cothen, *What Happened to the Southern Baptist Convention* (Macon GA: Smyth & Helwys, 1993), subtitled "A Memoir of the Controversy," it is written by one of the most important denominational leaders in the last half of the twentieth century, and it and Leonard's work are the best entries into the controversy for the novice. Nancy Tatom Ammerman, ed., *Southern Baptists Observed: Multiple Perspectives on a Changing Denomination* (Knoxville: University of Tennessee Press, 1993), contains the article mentioned above by Diane Winston and other excellent articles, especially the one by Samuel S. Hill. Walter B. Shurden, ed., *The Struggle for the Soul of the SBC: Moderate Responses to the Fundamentalist Movement* (Macon GA: Mercer University Press, 1993), includes extremely valuable chapters by some of the major moderate voices during the controversy such as Cecil Sherman, Daniel Vestal, Duke McCall, Glenn Hinson, Alan Neely, James Slatton, and others. Grady Cothen, *The New SBC: Fundamentalism's Impact on the Southern Baptist Convention* (Macon GA: Smyth & Helwys, 1995), an extremely valuable sequel to Cothen's 1993 book noted above.

[7]As quoted in "Criswell Says Patterson Won't Lead Inerrantists," Baptist Press, 9 May 1980, 6.

[8]See "Doctrinal Unity, Program Unity Rise, Fall Together, Rogers Says," Baptist Press, 14 May 1982, 6.

[9]Bill J. Leonard, *God's Last and Only Hope*, 138.

[10]As quoted in William S. Stone, Jr., "The Southern Baptist Convention Reformation, 1979–1990: A Social Drama" (Ph.D. dissertation, Louisiana State University, 1993) 73.

[11]I am indebted to William S. Stone, Jr., and his study of the controversy for stressing the importance of the 1979 SBC Pastor's Conference and the rhetorical dimension of the fundamentalist success. Anyone present at that meeting realizes the truth of Stone's contention. The rhetoric of the controversy has been too little noted as a crucial ingredient in the struggle.

[12]See "An Address to the Public from the Interim Steering Committee of the Cooperative Baptist Fellowship," in *The Struggle For the Soul of the SBC*, Walter B. Shurden, ed. (Macon GA: Mercer University Press, 1993) 312.

[13]As quoted in Winston, 21.

[14]Cecil E. Sherman, "An Overview of the Moderate Movement," in *The Struggle for the Soul of the SBC*, 41. For a copy of "The Glorieta Statement" see ibid., 295-96.

[15]For an extended analysis and historical treatment, see my article, "The Priesthood of All Believers and Pastoral Authority in Baptist Thought," *Faith and Mission* 7\1 (Fall 1989): 24-45.

[16]Paige Patterson, "My Vision of the Twenty-First Century SBC," *Review & Expositor* 88\1 (Winter 1991): 50.

[17]Cecil E. Sherman, "An Overview of the Moderate Movement," in *The Struggle for the Soul of the SBC*, 44.

[18]Samuel S. Hill, Jr., "The Shape and Shapes of Popular Southern Piety," in *Varieties of Southern Evangelicalism*, David E. Harrell, Jr., ed. (Macon GA: Mercer University Press, 1981) 99.

[19]Grady Cothen, *The New SBC*, 121-22. On this same point see Cecil Sherman's forthright indictment of those "who sat out the public part of the fight" in his "An Overview of the Moderate Movement," in *The Struggle for the Soul of the SBC*, 39-40, 43-44.

[20]Stone, 3.

[21]Cothen, *The New SBC*, 177.

[22]Ibid., 154-68.

[23]Ibid., 178.

Conclusion

Lessons from Baptist Controversies

The *facts* of history are not enough. We must learn the *lessons* of history, too. To make a denominational application: Baptists must do more than memorize the names, dates, and places of their yesterdays. We must learn the lessons that issue from the interaction of those hard-to-pronounce names, hard-to-remember dates, and hard-to-locate places. The study of history, as the study of the Bible, must be applied. In other words, there is a "so-what" element to the study of history.

Conflict and controversy have been at the very center of Baptist life. Indeed, I believe one could write a comprehensive and adequate denominational history by focusing only on the theme of controversy. Write a book entitled *Baptist Controversies*, and you have written a somewhat satisfactory summary of Baptist history. Baptists have squabbled from their very beginning—back in seventeenth-century England. They have argued over their history, their theology, their organization and church polity, the meaning of their ordinances, the missionary task of the church, and the social application of the gospel.

Throughout the chapters of this book I have tried to offer some interpretation of how the individual controversies have affected Southern Baptists. In these closing pages an enumeration of a few of the more general lessons to be learned from Baptist controversies may be helpful.

Lesson Number One

Controversy is inevitable among Baptists. Baptist life is built upon basic democratic principles that not only allow controversy; they encourage it. Baptist life has a strong stubborn streak of individualism. Look at the concept of faith: It is individualistic and personal. Each person must do one's own repenting. Each person accepts God's grace personally. Each comes "before God" on one's own. Look at the concept of the church: Each local congregation is free under Christ to run its own affairs. No outside organization, political or religious, can usurp the independence of the local church. Look at the aversion to creeds: Only sacred scriptures are normative for Baptists. We refuse to forfeit the freedom of biblical interpretation for the uniformity of any single theological statement. Look at the emphasis on religious liberty, separation of church and state, and the priesthood of all believers!

These ideas scream for freedom and issue in variety. One great Baptist soul said:

> The passion of the Baptists for liberty is one of their most strongly marked characteristics, flowing directly from the spiritual individualism which is their primary emphasis.[1]

Individualism demands freedom. Freedom creates diversity. Diversity inevitably leads to controversy.

Baptists could not avoid controversy. It was built into our major emphases. If you begin where Baptists begin—with individualism and freedom—you are driven to where Baptists are driven—controversy and conflict. On the other hand, if you begin wanting theological and doctrinal sameness, if you are fearful of differences and painful conflict, you will have to look elsewhere than to Baptists.

While contemporary Baptists often are portrayed as a parochial and narrow-minded group, narrow-mindedness had not been one of the salient characteristics of the Baptist tradition. Baptists are not nearly so much like King Frederick of Austria as some would have us believe. It was said of the king that he loved music, but not all music, just music played on a flute; but not all music played on a flute, just the music played on his own flute; but not all music played on his own flute, just the music that he played on his own flute!

While some Baptists—both past and present—have doubtless enjoyed only that music that they play on their own flutes, Baptist heritage has not usually issued a call for that kind of dedication to narrowness. Flexibility is built into the Baptist way of doing things. That flexibility produces diversity and conflict.

Lesson Number Two

Controversy is painful but often profitable. No one has made this point any better than John Clifford (1836–1923), one of the giants of English Baptist history. In 1888, a time of great theological and doctrinal unrest among English Baptists, Clifford preached a historic sermon that confronted and exposed rather than ignored and white-washed the controversy. Clifford quoted another Baptist who said, " 'The evils of controversy are all temporary, and its benefits are all permanent.' " Then Clifford added, "It is a consolatory message. We accept it with thankfulness; but it remains 'a hard saying.' "[2]

So true. It is "a hard saying" because controversy is painful. During denominational controversy there have always been those who, like the false prophets of the Old Testament, predict "Peace, peace, when there is no peace." They are not really false prophets. They are honest men and women who want to detour pain by detouring controversy. It cannot be done—at least not always, for denominations, like little boys with legaches, have "growing pains." They hurt, but it is better to hurt and grow than to never hurt and never grow.

John Clifford said,

Controversy is far better than stagnation. Even strife is a sign of vitality —uncomfortable, irritating vitality, perhaps; exceedingly disagreeable to fossil theologians and actual tyrants; but still it is vitality. He is not the typical Christian who is forever hugging the shores in search of the quietist harbors, but he who braves the storm and tempest with his lifeboat that he may save. Living men differ. It is the dead who agree. God educates His Church, if I may say it, by the Socratic method.[3]

Controversy has been exceedingly profitable for the Baptist denomination. The Whitsitt Controversy not only intensified interest in Baptist history; it delivered us from erroneous ideas. The controversy among English Baptists concerning the missionary responsibility of the churches launched the modern missionary movement, not just among Baptists but all religious bodies.

It is said that Mexican villagers who assume the worst is to be expected, often bid so-long to departing travelers with the blessing, "May you go with God, and may nothing new happen to you." Impossible! When people "go with God," new things happen. They are more often than not controversial and painful, and quite often they are profitable. So one should not pray that a denomination be delivered from all wrangling.

Yet, this is no call to embrace the new and novel indiscriminately; nor is it a call to arms, thinking that if we do battle we shall "grow up" as a denomination. Wayne E. Oates wisely observed that either to deify or to deny the past has disastrous results for a person. So it is with a denomination. Somehow we must learn to live in the terrible tension between what "was" and what "is."

Lesson Three

Controversy is often embodied in powerful personalities. This is true of controversy of any kind, but it is especially true of Baptist controversy. Because Baptists have refused to commit themselves to official creeds, authoritative church manuals, or ecclesiastical laws—things to which they could turn for final answers in a time of controversy—they have been left to follow the person with the eloquent voice, the power of persuasion, the genius of leadership, and/or the courage to voice a new conviction.

The power of personality is evident when one looks at the names of certain Baptist controversies. We have had the "Whitsitt" Controversy, the "Elliott" Controversy, and the "Norris" Controversy. Even when the controversy did not assume the name of one of its central figures, one can hardly think of a Baptist conflict without thinking of certain names. Spurgeon is associated with the "Downgrade" Controversy, J. R. Graves with the "Landmark" Controversy, and Daniel Parker and John Taylor with the "Anti-Missions" Controversy.

There is both a positive and a negative lesson here. The positive lesson is the fact that quite often very good and stalwart Christian leaders have advocated opposite points of view. Persons differed because they honestly held divergent interpretations on an issue and not because they had "ulterior motives," lacked "integrity," or some such. The negative lesson is the fact that controversy often degenerates into silly name-calling and demolishes the ministry and career of a good person. This has happened in Baptist history.

While controversy is most often embodied in powerful personalities, it should not become "personal." To label a person a "liberal," "fundamentalist," "radical," "activist" is too often an excuse for not using hard, critical thinking and a way of confessing that one lacks the patience to listen. Labels should be for identifying point of view; they are frequently used to accuse and indict. Our opinions may be wrong; our courtesy, fairness, and love will never be.

Lesson Four

A controversy is never finally and absolutely settled among Baptists—and for a very good reason. There is no person, persons, or organization from whom a final word can come in Baptist life. Baptists have often issued confessions of faith and public statements. These documents were directed toward a particular question, but they only indicated the point of view of a majority of Baptists at a particular time. These do not become binding on all Baptists. Baptists have consistently refused to be restricted by anything that smacked of creedalism.

One of the clearest examples of this attitude is to be found in the confession of faith adopted by the Southern Baptist Convention in 1925. The reason for the confession was "the prevalence of naturalism in the modern teaching" and specifically the idea of evolution. The committee that drafted and presented the confession of faith also presented a statement on the nature and functions of confessions of faith among Baptists. The committee members said they did not regard confessional documents "as complete statements of our faith, having any quality of finality or infallibility." Moreover, "confessions are only guides in interpretation, having no authority over the conscience."

Occasionally you may hear a distraught Baptist say of a lingering denominational agitation, "Let's forget that argument; we settled that years ago." Rest assured that he or she is wrong. Nothing is ever finally and irrevocably settled among Baptists. This is part of the Baptist genius.

The above are four lessons from Baptist controversies, but one certainly cannot say: "Here endeth the lessons." The centrality of Baptist newspapers, the fact that theological controversy often is settled with the big stick of a financial boycott (the we'll-stop-giving syndrome), the fact that personality conflicts give rise to denominational disputes—these are a few of the "other" lessons one could point to in Baptist controversies.

When you study Baptist history, you will understand that the old adage that says "anytime you find two Baptists you will find three ideas" is not far from true. The Baptist denominational consciousness has been fostered more by the unity that comes from a commitment to diversity than by the unity that comes from uniformity.

Notes

[1]H. Wheeler Robinson, *The Life and Faith of the Baptists* (London: Carey Kingsgate Press, Ltd., 1946) 123.

[2]As quoted in Sydnor L. Stealey, *A Baptist Treasury* (New York: Thomas Y. Crowell Co., 1958) 98.

[3]Ibid., 98-101.